iPhone 15 (

An Illustrated and Simple-to-Follow Guide for Beginners: A Quick and Easy Way to Master Your New iPhone 15 Pro & pro Max Wonders

Chris Amber

Table of Contents

PREFACE

Discover the Full Potential of Your iPhone 15 with Our Detailed User Guide Book!

Are you prepared to enhance your iPhone 15 experience further? There's nowhere else to look! Our unique user guide book is made to improve your iPhone skills and serve readers worldwide.

Inside:

- Thorough explanation of the features and capabilities of the iphone 15.

- Advice on how to get the most out of your gadget.

- Detailed instructions for learning how to use the newest iOS releases.

- Discover the possibilities of state-of-the-art technology at your fingertips!

Why Select Our User Manual?

- *Worldwid4e Reach:* Our guide is ideal for people everywhere because it is not limited by language.

- *User-friendly:* Our tutorial is designed for all levels of experience, from novices to IT enthusiasts.

- *Visually captivating:* Rich with eye-catching pictures and graphics that make understanding simple.

- *Regular upgrades:* Keep up with the most recent improvements and upgrades for the iphone 15.

Go Beyond Your iPhone 15 with These Handpicked Suggestions:

- *Samsung S23:* Experience Android with the newest innovation from Samsung.

- ☑ *Unlock iPhone XS and iPhone XR* to explore an infinite array of options by selecting your own carrier.

- 🛡 *Privacy Screen Protector for iPhone 14 Pro:* Protect your privacy with cutting-edge safeguards.

- 💼 *For the best possible device protection*, combine style and durability with the Spigen iPhone 14 Pro Max Case.

- 🚀 **Unlocked iPhone 13 Pro Max:** Unrestrictedly use the full capability of your iPhone 13!

🌼 Adorn and Safeguard:

- *Spigen iPhone 14 Pro Case:* Up your style game with this stylish case.

- 🛡 *Protector Para iPhone 14 Pro Max:* We've got you covered if you speak Spanish! 🔒

- *iPhone 14 Plus Privacy Screen:* Protect your screen from snoopers.

🔒 Activate a Universe of Opportunities:

- *Unlocked iPhone 11 Pro Max:* Unrestricted access to global networks.

- 🚀 *Boost Infinite:* Enhance your iPhone experience and increase connectivity.

↤ *Grow Your Apple Network:*

- 🍎 *Apple Watch:* For a connected lifestyle, seamlessly integrate your wearable technology.

- 📺 *Apple TV:* Upgrade your viewing pleasure with the company's newest TV innovation.

Upgrading to the iPhone 15 and Later:

- 📱 iPhone 14, iPhone SE, iPhone 13, iPhone 13 Mini Unlocked: Keep up with the newest iPhone models to stay technologically advanced.

- 🌼 Take in the ultimate Apple experience with the Apple Max.

📞 Get Your Copy Now to Explore the Next Frontier of iPhone Technology! 🚀 🗄

Get in quick, while supplies last! 👻 Globally accessible. ✳

INTRODUCTION

Get an iPhone 15 but also a handbook that teaches you how to make the most of all of its amazing features. If you settle for anything less, you won't be able to fully utilize this incredible smartphone.

Get ready for the next wave of smartphone innovation. The much anticipated iPhone 15 is about to change how we use our phones. Modern features and technology are anticipated to make the iPhone 15 the most cutting-edge and inventive smartphone to date. With its improved camera features and longer battery life (Which help you not to carry Power Banks around), the iPhone 15 is expected to have a big impact on the mobile device market.

Presenting the much awaited iPhone 15! With its most recent release, which is jam-packed with cutting-edge features and technology, Apple has lifted the bar once more. With its sophisticated camera features, improved performance, and stylish new appearance, the iPhone 15 has raised the bar for smartphones.

"iPhone 15 Manual" is a guidebook written with the inexperienced user in mind, not just a handbook. Our goal is to demystify each feature and convey it in an easy-to-understand manner. We'll walk you through exploring the technological wonders of your smartphone using simple language and clear visuals, making the learning experience entertaining as well as instructive.

Discover how to use your iPhone's amazing cameras to capture incredibly gorgeous images and movies.

With its remarkable assortment of seven professional-grade lenses, 48MP Main camera, new camera modes, astounding 24MP default resolution, special 5x Telephoto camera, and numerous other new camera capabilities, the new iPhone 15 series camera is brimming with never-before-seen features on a smartphone.

This extensive user manual explores all of the capabilities that make use of the iPhone camera, including the FaceTime, Photos, and Camera apps. You'll learn how to unleash your creative potential by learning how to position and adjust your camera for the perfect picture and video capture.

This book aims to provide you comfort, familiarity, and comprehension with your device so that you can explore with confidence rather than overwhelming you with technical terms or cliches.

Explore the world of apps in great detail, learn the meaning behind features, and master the iPhone 15. The pictorial guide will not only pique your curiosity but also inspire you to discover and utilize the cutting-edge capabilities of your gadget, which will make daily chores more enjoyable and effective. This guide covers everything, from configuring your new iPhone to comprehending the settings, making the most of the camera, and protecting your security and privacy. The icing on the cake are the extra tips and tricks that guarantee you are making the most of your iPhone hassle-free.

Enjoy your new iPhone 15 to the fullest and don't let your fear of technology get in the way! Take a deep dive into this thorough and detailed guide to master your gadget.

A few of the topics this manual covers are as follows:

- The iPhone 15 & 15 Plus's components

- The LiDAR Scanner's operation

- Establishment Process

- iCloud Profile

- How to Utilize the Phone Locator Feature

- Introducing the features of iOS 17

- Discover the iPhone 15 Series' innovative photography features.

- Discover the techniques for taking breathtaking images in low light and extending your dynamic range using Smart HDR and Night mode.

- Learn the techniques of expert photo editing to create truly amazing images from your photos.

- With the help of cutting-edge Depth and Control Focus technology, your portrait photography will soar.

- How to initialize your Apple Pay account

- How to use Apple Pay with a credit or debit card

- How to make contactless payments with Apple Pay

- How to locate locations that use Apple Pay using Siri

- How a gift card is used

- How to use Safari's Apple Pay feature

- Crucial Elements in the Entire Series: Examine the unique qualities that make the iPhone 15 series unique.

- File Transfer from Android to iPhone 15: Ensure a seamless and trouble-free move.

- Using Picture-in-Picture mode to multitask can increase productivity.

- Sync your data between devices with ease by using the iCloud Settings.

- Activate this function by using the Action Button.

- Aligning Camera Shooting Angle: Sharpen your photographic techniques to produce jaw-dropping images.

- Use Night Shift to lessen eye strain and enhance the quality of your sleep.

- Configuring and Personalizing Siri: Customize Siri to meet your needs!...and our guide has a lot more in store for you!

Don't allow doubt stop you from using your smartphone to its fullest capacity. Stay tuned for more information on this exciting new product's debut and upgrades. Continue reading to get all the fascinating specifics of this revolutionary gadget.

Learn about the ultimate iPhone adventure! Explore the world of innovation and protect your gadget with premium add-ons. Our carefully chosen collection ensures an unmatched, immersive iPhone experience, whether it's exploring the possibilities of your iPhone 15 or embracing the stylish design of the iPhone XS and XR, protecting privacy with the iPhone 14 Plus privacy screen protector, or enjoying better audio with Raycon earphones. With the ideal balance of practicality and flair, you can improve your safety, show off your style, and stay up to date with technology!

CHAPTER 1

Updates on the iPhone 15's specifications, cost, and launch date

The iPhone 15 was revealed on September 12, 2023. Preorders are accepted right now, and shipping begins on September 22. Numerous updates have been made to this edition, including the switch to USB-C, the addition of an Action button reminiscent of the Apple Watch, slimmer bezels, Dynamic Island for all versions, and titanium Pro variants.

Key characteristics of the iPhone 15 and 15 Plus

The iPhone 15 is offered in four versions, like it did last year: iPhone 15, 15 Plus, 15 Pro, and 15 Pro Max. The screens on the 15 and Pro are 6.1 inches, while the screens on the Plus and Pro Max are 6.7 inches.

There are tons of amazing features and options in the new

iPhone 15 series. Here are a few noteworthy ones that Apple revealed at the launch event:

- A fresh layout featuring the Dynamic Island, which grows and changes in response to your actions. For instance, you can use it to simultaneously manage music, view instructions, and monitor deliveries and sports scores.

- Thinner boundaries and support for Dolby Vision.

- Extremely powerful A16 core CPU

- A GPU with five cores is great for graphics and games.

- Reaches a brightness of 1600 nits, reaching 2000 nits in direct sunlight.

- Resistance to water.

- 75% recyclable aluminum with 100% recycled copper foil.

- Completely new, cutting-edge camera system: a 48 megapixel primary camera and a 12 megapixel telephoto lens that provide high-resolution portrait possibilities and continuous zoom even in dim or dusk light.

- The iPhone 15 boasts an upgraded ultra-wideband with a second-generation chip that enhances precise position finding, ideal for locating loved ones.

- Speech Isolation: A machine learning algorithm that gives priority to your speech over other sounds, resulting in improved audio quality.

- SOS for emergencies: Extended to 14 nations across 3 continents.

- Roadside assistance with satellite: With AAA, you may get moving from anywhere at any time with a fast text that directs you to a satellite (needs AAA membership; free for two years with iPhone 15).

- USB-C connector for data transfer and charging. AirPods, iPad, iPhone, and Mac are all charged by this as well.

- To make it easier to align your phone with a

wireless charger, use MagSafe.

iPhone 15   iPhone 15 Pro

Highlights of the iPhone 15 Pro and Pro Max Features

All the features of the iPhone 15 are available on the iPhone 15 Pro/Pro+ models, but they go one step further:

- A17 Pro, the first 3-nanometer chip in the industry With microarchitectural and design advancements, the new CPU is up to 10% quicker, and the Neural Engine—which powers iOS 17's autocorrect and Personal Voice features—is now up to 2 times faster.

- Click the action button. This takes the role of the Mute/Silence switch, however it will still function as such by default. You may configure the Action Button to do a number of tasks, such as launching the camera app, initiating a shortcut, or even turning on the flashlight.

- A titanium design with recycled aluminum inside that employs grade 5 titanium, which is extraordinarily robust and durable but incredibly lightweight.

- The thinnest iPhone boundaries ever

- Available in 6.1" and 6.7" sizes.

- Four colors are possible with a PVD exterior coating: White, Black, Blue, and Natural (uncolored Titanium).

- An internal chassis architecture that makes it easy to repair the phone.

- ProMotion: The new, extremely high-resolution 24MP default capture is now supported by the 48MP main camera system. The system includes features including Night mode upgrades, Focus and

Depth Control for the next generation of portraiture, and Smart HDR.

- When the phone is on standby—which is a fully customizable experience—it is rotated horizontally and charges.

- Pro Performance: A brand-new A17 Pro chip made with a novel 3-nanometer manufacturing technique. Two high-performance cores and four high-efficiency cores make up the new A17 Pro's six core CPU. Now, the GPU has six cores.

- Ten gigabit per second (Gbps) of transfer speed is possible with a USB-C connector and a USB 3 controller (20 times faster than prior generations).

- Energy-efficient gaming features include hardware-based ray tracing to reflect gaming environments faster than ever (4 times faster), better resolution for higher-quality features, MetalFX scaling to provide more detailed gaming environments, and mesh shading for better graphics that use less power.

- Multiple lenses, the longest optical zoom ever with

Focus and Depth Control, enhancements to Night mode and Smart HDR, and an entirely new 5x Telephoto camera available only on the iPhone 15 Pro Max comprise a pro camera system. This features a 5X mm telephoto camera with a 120 mm lens and a 12MP Ultra Wide camera with a 10x optical zoom capability.

- Ability to record spatial video for use on the Apple Vision Pro.

When Is the iPhone 15 Coming Out?

The iPhone 15 Pro and iPhone 15 Pro Max went on sale on Friday, September 22, and pre-orders started on September 15.

There will be four color options for the iPhone 15 Pro and iPhone 15 Pro Max: black, white, blue, and natural titanium.

Pricing of the iPhone 15 and iPhone 15 Pro

The iPhone 15 starts at $799, while the Plus starts at $899. There are three different storage options: 128GB, 256GB, or 512GB.

There are four storage options for the iPhone 15 Pro: 128GB, 256GB, 512GB, and 1TB. It costs $999.

Starting at $1,199, the iPhone 15 Pro Max comes in three storage options: 256GB, 512GB, and 1TB.

With a new subscription, customers who buy the iPhone 15 Pro or iPhone 15 Pro Max will receive three months of free access to Apple Arcade and Apple Fitness+.

Another Typical Apple Surprise Is the iPhone 15 Pro Max's Tetraprism Camera

One of the more clever revelations from Apple in recent memory is the new tetraprism 'zoom' lens seen in the iPhone 15 Pro Max. Apple excels at taking an established concept and turning it into something new.

Tetraprisms are similar to periscope lenses, however instead of spinning a long tube of lenses to run the length of the iPhone, they are formed by folding a prism into waves. It's a really clever concept that will increase the flexibility of the iPhone camera system.

"With an aperture of 2.8 and a focal length of 120mm, this lens is going to be a serious portrait lens. It will create real background blur, not the artificial kind that can look unnatural," replied travel photographer Tom Bourdon in an email interview with Lifewire. "I imagine many photographers will upgrade to this mobile simply because of this lens."

Go Live on Periscope

Periscope lens rumors have surrounded the iPhone for years, but now that it's official, it's even more intriguing than anticipated. Let's examine its necessity first, then move on to how it functions.

You may have seen the large camera turret protruding out the rear of a current iPhone Pro model if you have used one. It is there to support ever-larger lenses—which are required for the larger camera sensors—and to expand the iPhone's camera array's telephoto capabilities. However, as we can see, the turret is currently absurdly large and won't be able to become much bigger before being completely unusable.

A periscope lens is precisely what you would expect it to be. It runs the length of the iPhone rather than protruding perpendicularly from the back panel, allowing the lens to be longer. It does this by using prisms to reflect incoming light across a 90-degree angle. This design's drawback is that it requires more internal room in the camera.

Apple is applying the periscope concept without twisting it to a 90-degree angle. Rather, four links have been inserted into an internal prism, each of which folds light to make the light path longer while maintaining alignment with the other conventional lenses.

The fact that all of these kinks are contained within a single tetraprism simplifies matters and might help explain why the lens appears to not absorb too much light, leading to that bright (at least for this focal length) maximum aperture of 2.8.

A glass prism can have exceptional optical quality. Pentaprisms, or glass blocks that reflect incoming light off five internal surfaces and bring it to your eye, are used in the viewfinders of high-quality SLR and DSLR cameras. The large angled viewfinder piece on top of the camera contains that.

iPhone Lens Reach

What then is the potential of a 120mm lens? The natural response is that the additional magnification allows you to get closer to the subject. Although you won't be able to select your child out of the entire cast of their upcoming school play, you can zoom in close to get rid of most of the distracting background.

This kind of long telephoto lens works well for portraiture as well. A subject appears more distorted in the frame the closer you approach to them. Get up close to someone else's face, close one eye, and observe how strange their features appear from this vantage point. Bulbous nose, receding cheeks, etc. Wide-angle lenses necessitate coming near to the subject, which is why they are so unattractive.

This is not the case with the telephoto lens. It enables you to take frame-filling pictures from a greater distance, resulting in far more attractive pictures. A subject is also naturally separated from everything behind them by a longer lens, which likewise blurs the background more than a wide lens does.

Additionally, the quality is far greater because there is no "digital zoom" involved—rather, the magnification is purely optical—rather than merely cropping the image to highlight the center.

Let's end with a rumor, since we began with one. The 15 Pro Max is currently the only iPhone with a tetraprism lens, but that will change the next year. If you're not like large phones, you can wait a year before replacing your phone if supply-chain sources claim that the standard iPhone 16 will gain this fantastic feature.

For many people, especially those who shoot a lot of pictures, this single-camera boost may be enough to justify purchasing a new phone. If not, wait, since this is most likely how iPhone cameras will look in the future.

Ray Tracing's Possible Advantages for iPhone 15 Gamers

Soon, the next iPhone may mimic the functionality of a game console.

The latest A17 Pro chip, designed with improved GPU capabilities in mind, powers the iPhone 15 Pro. Apple asserts that the new 6-core design of this state-of-the-art "pro-class" GPU improves performance while simultaneously decreasing power consumption. By introducing hardware-accelerated ray tracing, the gadget claims to have GPU performance that is up to 20% quicker than before.

"Ray tracing provides better level design, better gameplay and, as a result—better user experience," said Pavel Shkarpenin, platform relations manager at MY.GAMES, in an email interview with Lifewire. "Apple has been saying for years that we can expect unprecedented quality and gameplay in our pocket—and to be able to bring an ultra-realistic feel to games through advanced lighting techniques like ray tracing means Apple can more effectively deliver on that promise."

Is That an Apple Game Phone?

Some of the AAA titles that will be available on the recently announced iPhone 15 Pro include Assassin's Creed Mirage, Resident Evil 4 Remake, Resident Evil Village, Death Stranding, and a slew of others. For an even better iPhone gaming experience, Apple boasted of major performance upgrades and the use of ray tracing.

"The combination of incredible iOS optimization and Apple silicon performance make new iPhones better for gaming than they ever have been before," stated Shkarpenin. "While we didn't see a 120Hz (or even 90Hz) refresh rate on the cheaper iPhone 15, their inclusion on the flagship 15 Pro and Max models make both of these exciting prospects."

In addition to the A17 Pro's revolutionary architecture and

upscaling, Ray Tracing—a lighting method that adds an extra degree of realism to games—will be crucial, according to Shkarpenin.

"Mobile gaming relies heavily on the ability to be efficient because you are using your phone for other things, and you are not necessarily playing while connected to a power outlet every day, which degrades battery life," according to him.

Nate Amaral, branding and communications coordinator at gaming startup ExitLag, said in an email that the new A17 Pro processor, which is part of the Pro lineup on iPhone 15, has two primary improvements for gaming: two additional GPU cores and the integration of Apple's Neural Engine with the GPU. According to him, this indicates that Apple is following Nvidia's lead and seeking to improve performance and efficiency by utilizing the GPU's architecture.

"Heavy graphic games, like Asphalt 9 or Genshin Impact, will see not only better graphics but better performance and battery consumption, making the push into 60/120 frames per second in an iPhone 15 Pro / 15 Pro Max a feasible reality," according to him. "The new iPhone 15 GPU brings more quality of life for gamers all over the board."

In an email, Steve Athwal, managing director of The Big Phone Store, highlighted how the components of the A17 Pro chip will enhance its gaming powers.

"For gaming, the key components will be the GPU and NPU, as these work together to deliver processor-intensive gaming graphics quickly," according to him. The Neural engine replicates the functionality of DLSS on an Nvidia RTX graphics card by functioning as a 'upscaler' when playing games. This enables the GPU to 'upscale' images from lower resolutions to higher ones, and by playing the game at a lower native resolution, the GPU can function at a considerably faster speed.

What Lies Ahead for iPhones Video game

Improvements to iPhone gaming may be on the horizon. Amaral stated that the most intriguing potential is that Apple would likely introduce the new GPU Architecture,

Ray Tracing, and Upscaling for its M3 lineup, which uses the A/A Pro chip series.

"We can expect M3 Macs and iPads with even better graphics and GPU calculations, which, together with the industry's crescent adoption of ARM/Mobile architecture, paves the way for Apple to be a serious gaming competitor," according to him.

The new iPhone might be able to take on products like the Logitech G Cloud or Valve Steam Deck with its combination of a top-notch screen and a new chip. For the time being, though, Windows PCs will continue to have the largest selection of games available to serious gamers.

The New Spatial Videos on the iPhone 15 Pro Are a Fantastic Present for Your Future Self.

Capture breathtaking 3D video with the iPhone 15 Pro by using the Vision Pro augmented reality eyewear. Furthermore, it will progressively change your life.

Those of you who own an iPhone may be familiar with

and fond of Live Photos, which record a short video clip—complete with audio—to accompany each photo. You might have Live Photos of friends and family members going back eight years, since these have been available since the iPhone 6S in 2015. If you want to remember the person's movements and voice from years ago, these are far more effective than a standard still image. The new spatial picture and video capabilities are going to make that seem a lot more genuine.

"Live Photos on the iPhone always did more than capture images for me—they captured moments," says Maxwell Bentley, CEO of Bentley Media and a video producer. Enjoying a brief video clip of my fiancée laughing as we take a photo together, a breathtaking sunset over the Atlanta cityscape, or vacation highlights is one of my favorite things to do when I browse back over my feed. I can't wait to see how far the iPhone 15's Spatial Video capability takes this.

I Appreciate the Recollections

Give this mental exercise a go if you've worked with Live Photos before. Bring to mind an experience from a very long time ago. Just before your little one figured out how to open the kitchen saucepan drawer, it may be their first few toddling steps. It may be a snapshot from your own youth, a picture of your first romantic partner, or even a house that you adored but no longer live in.

Imagine if those moments were captured in real-time through photos. Being able to see those individuals move would be amazing, wouldn't it? Remember what they sounded like? As far as those old enough to remember their formative years are concerned, that is precisely how it will play out.

This is heading somewhere, and you already know it. Envision now that these recollections are accessible in three dimensions. As a kid, you can sit on the floor beside yourself while wearing Apple's Vision Pro headset. Either a 3D spatial video or a still 3D image with rotating or otherwise adjustable viewpoints could be here. Just picture yourself reliving those magical experiences from your life in this way. I find that quite astounding.

The development of more advanced forms of immersive

media, such as Apple's Vision Pro, holds great potential for the future of memory preservation and reliving. According to graphic designer and tech expert Sanef Safwan, "the potential for enriching our connection with memories is evident in these innovations," but whether or not this becomes the killer feature for the iPhone Vision Pro depends on individual preferences.

Social Media or Vision Pro?

When Apple presented a father video his kids playing together with the 3D cameras in the Vision Pro headset during the launch event, it was a rare PR gaffe. The internet thinks it was scary because the dystopic hat blocked dad from seeing his kids.

It is wonderful that the iPhone 15 Pro can now record spatial audio and video since, as everyone knows, a parent who is absorbed in their phone is far more in the here and now. Even if you won't be able to see it in 3D until the Vision Pro is available for purchase at an unknown future date, isn't $3,500 worth it for the memories it will preserve?

Besides being more convenient, capturing from a phone also begs the question of potential uses for the captures. Making a social media post about them is a very real option.

"Living through the memories again would be more exciting. It will be fascinating to observe the impact on video-sharing platforms like Instagram, YouTube, TikTok, and others. I'm even more thrilled about that! Envision yourself fully immersed in a mountaintop experience while viewing a hiking movie shot by your beloved photographer. "Nothing beats that," Asmita Kunwar, proprietor of a fashion line and an Instagram influencer, proudly revealed.

We have no guarantee that the Vision Pro will be successful or that its price will eventually fall to a level where we can purchase it. However, you ought to begin recording spatial memories without a doubt if you purchase a new iPhone 15 Pro. I mean, you never know. Consider it a wonderful present for the you of tomorrow.

The iPhone 15's cameras come equipped with

enhanced low-light performance, automatic portrait mode, and other features as standard.

During its most recent Wonderlust event, Apple largely showcased the capabilities of the new iPhone 15 line's improved cameras, which are a significant improvement above what the firm gave on the iPhone 14.

The first noticeable change is the upgraded camera sensor from 12 megapixels on the previous generation to 48 megapixels on the new iPhone 15. Apple claims that the 24-megapixel photographs produced by the primary camera provide "incredible" picture quality without consuming excessive storage space. A 2x telephoto mode is also available by cropping the sensor's middle 12 megapixels. For the first time in Apple's more cheap handset series, the iPhone 15 and iPhone 15 Plus provide three levels of zoom—0.5x, 1x, and 2x. If you ever want to get every detail of a scene, you can switch to the dedicated wide-angle lens.

Improvements to Apple's computational photography software back up the new hardware. To get photos with bokeh effects, for example, you can utilize any camera app's regular Portrait Mode. The iPhone 15 can automatically take depth information when you tap on a topic, which it may then utilize to blur the background. After taking a picture, you can even change the focus. Apple also claims that Night Mode will have crisper details and more vibrant colors. The business has also improved its Smart HDR feature so that it can deal with illumination that isn't uniform.

The Pro and Max models of the iPhone 15 naturally have all the improvements to the camera quality that were available on the iPhone 15 and more. Apple claims that its new flagships include seven professional lenses' worth of features. You may choose between a 24mm, 28mm, or 35mm lens with the 48-megapixel main camera on the iPhone 15 and 15 Pro Max. In addition, the new telephoto camera on both phones has a 5x optical zoom and a 120mm lens. Although it's not the most zoom-friendly feature on the market, it is the most ever supplied by Apple in a mobile device. The new tetraprism design on the iPhone 15 Pro and 15 Pro Max, according to the company, also includes its most advanced optical image stabilization capability.

The two phones will receive an update from Apple later this year that adds functionality for spatial video capturing. This feature will be useful when the company's Vision Pro headset arrives. You may pre-order any iPhone 15 starting on Friday, September 15, and then you can buy one in stores starting on September 22.

The iPhone 15 Now Features USB-C, a Dynamic Island, 48MP, and Gorgeous Colors

The iPhone with USB-C has arrived. Today during its 'Wonderlust' event in Cupertino, California, Apple revealed the iPhone 15. As anticipated, the business has shifted to using USB-C instead of its proprietary Lightning connector, and both of the new iPhone 15 versions use the new port. This implies that connecting the new iPhones to a variety of gadgets, such as Apple's MacBook computers, will be simpler for users. However, it also means outdated Lightning accessories won't operate with the iPhone 15 without an adaptor. Conveniently, the switch to USB-C ensures that the new iPhones abide by impending EU legislation aimed at reducing electronic waste.

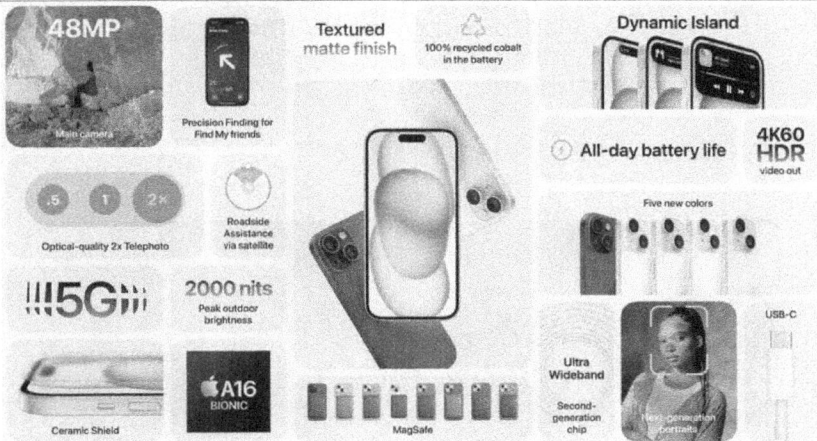

Similar to the iPhone 14 series, Apple will release the iPhone 15 in two sizes: 6.1 inches and 6.7 inches. The latter will continue to use the 'Plus' branding from the previous edition. The Dynamic Island display cutout, which Apple debuted in 2022, is new on the iPhone 15. That capability was limited to the iPhone 14 Pro and iPhone 14 Pro Max earlier.

Additionally, Apple fitted the iPhone 15 with a new Super Retina OLED screen, which has a brightness of 1,600 nits and can display HDR content. The new screen can reach a maximum brightness of 2,000 nits in sunny weather, which is twice as bright as the iPhone 14's display. The A16 Bionic technology, which Apple first unveiled with the iPhone 14 Pro last year, is also included with the two new iPhone 15 versions. With its most recent pair of mainstream smartphones, Apple is also boasting "all-day" battery life thanks to a larger battery.

Kaiann Drance
VP, iPhone Product Marketing

The iPhone 15 boasts a whole new primary camera array with a 12-megapixel telephoto lens and a 48-megapixel primary sensor for photographers. If it sounds similar, it's because Apple switched to the iPhone 14, which has a 48-megapixel camera. The iPhone 15's front camera features portrait lighting and autofocus for those who love taking selfies.

The new phones will be available from the company in a variety of vibrant colors, including Pink, Blue, Green, Yellow, and Black. This Friday, September 15, Apple will start taking preorders for the iPhone 15, with a September release date for wide availability. The iPhone 15 is priced starting at $799. Meanwhile, iPhone 15 Plus pricing will begin at $899.

Separately, Apple declared that on Monday, September 18, the upcoming iOS 17 version of its mobile operating system will be available as a free update. After revealing iOS 17 at its yearly WWDC conference in June, the Apple has been testing the new software in public. A number of new features will be included in the upgrade, such as a customizable call screen makeover and Check-In, which notifies reliable contacts when you've reached your location safely.

Although the iPhone 15 Pro still costs $999, its camera is better than ever.

At its 'Wonder lust' event in California, Apple just unveiled the iPhone 15 Pro, which comes with a number of improvements.

With a revolutionary grade-five titanium construction, the iPhone 15 Pro weighs less than any previous iPhone model. Apple says that because of a unique PVD coating, it's also their most durable phone to date. As previously, Apple will provide the Pro in two variants: a 6.1-inch model and a 6.7-inch 'Max' model. Additionally, the iPhone Pro's interior design has been altered by the business to increase its repairability and utilization of recycled materials. The iPhone 14 Pro has a new 'Action Button' in place of the previous ringer switch. The button can be configured by users to do specific functions. You may set up the button to start recording a voice memo, for example. It can also launch the camera app, activate the phone's flashlight, and do a lot more. Additionally, Apple is releasing a new standby display mode, which turns on when the phone is placed on a wireless charger in a landscape configuration.

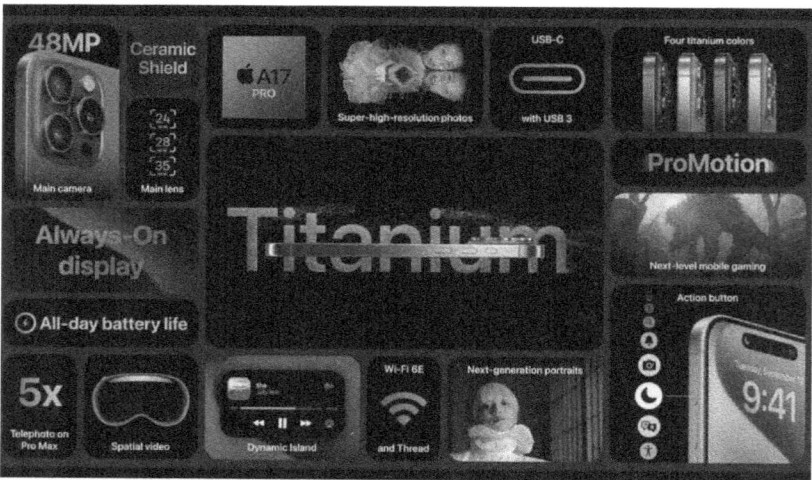

The new 3-nanometer A17 Pro chipset from Apple is housed inside the iPhone 15 Pro. The two high-performance cores on the new chip, according to the manufacturer, are 10% faster than those on the previous model. The integrated neural engine is also up to two times faster. In addition to being quicker, the GPU of the A17 Pro is capable of hardware-based ray tracing, which will enable game developers to include more lifelike lighting in their products.

While the A17 Pro has a specialized USB controller that allows 10Gbps data transfers, the iPhone 15 Pro also has USB-C connectivity. Naturally, Apple has also made significant updates to the iPhone 15 Pro's camera system. It boasts an upgraded 48-megapixel main camera that Apple claims is better at shooting low-light photographs and is less subject to lens flare (sorry, J.J. Abrams). Users of the camera can also alter the focus length. You may take pictures with focal lengths of 24 mm, 28 mm, and 35 mm. In addition, the telephoto camera comes with a 120mm focal length and an optical zoom of up to 5x.

Pre-orders for the iPhone 15 Pro and Pro Max will open on September 15. For the 128GB variant, the former starts at $999, while the latter starts at $1,119. On September 22, shipping will begin.

Separately, Apple declared that on Monday, September 18, the upcoming iOS 17 version of its mobile operating system will be available as a free update. After revealing iOS 17 at its yearly WWDC conference in June, the Apple has been testing the new software in public. A number of new features will be included in the upgrade, such as a customizable call screen makeover and Check-In, which notifies reliable contacts when you've reached your location safely.

CHAPTER 2

Utilization of the Apple iPhone 15 Pro in Practice

The A17 Pro chip, ultra-thin borders, Action button, USB-C port, Titanium finish, and iOS 17 out of the box are all features of the Apple iPhone 15 Pro. For the past week or so, I've been using the 15 Pro (1TB model) as my main smartphone, and aside from a little initial uncertainty (I'm more used to Android smartphones), I had a terrific experience.

Create and Present

Natural titanium, blue titanium, white titanium, and black titanium are the five colors available for the attractive and lightweight titanium smartphone known as the iPhone 15 Pro.

Slightly larger than the iPhone 14 Pro, the 6.1-inch display is covered with Ceramic Shield, a type of glass that, according to Apple, delivers four times the protection of rival smartphone glass.

It features Apple's Dynamic Island, which is a pill-shaped box at the top of the screen that shows notifications and running tasks (such timers or Map directions), just like the 14 Pro.

What's New?

The biggest modification is the move from Lightning to USB-C connectors for accessories and charging. You can also charge wirelessly with Qi-compatible chargers and Apple's MagSafe charging pad.

Additionally, the Action button added to the Pro model (which is still present on the iPhone 15 and 15 Plus) takes the place of the earlier models' Mute switch. It has the most recent Apple A17 Pro chip (as of 2023) installed.

Standby Mode, a new feature of iOS 17, allows you to use your lock screen to show a widget—like a huge clock—while it charges on your nightstand.

The iPhone 15, iPhone 15 Plus, iPhone 15 Pro, and the flagship iPhone 15 Pro Max are the four iterations of the iPhone 15 that Apple has launched.

Cameras, Features, and Performance

Even with numerous apps open, the iPhone 15 responds well and allows for fast app switching. FaceID was new to me, so I expected it to be difficult. (It's not an option on the Pro, but I prefer to use my fingerprint.) Fortunately, I was mistaken; without any effort at all, the screen unlocked at several angles right away.

I expect to see more development of the Action button, a cool new hardware feature, in next software releases. The phone goes into silent mode by default when the button, which is situated above the volume controls on the left side, is held down. That said, you can configure it to do a number of things, such as turning on your flashlight, recording a voice memo, and triggering a shortcut.

Instead of forcing you to choose only one action, I envisage future versions letting you select several (maybe with a short push or double press).

The iPhone 15 Pro has three cameras: a 3X zoom lens, an ultra-wide lens, and a 48MP primary camera. (The 5X periscope zoom lens on the 15 Pro Max.) It's a great addition that you can now utilize Portrait Mode on already-taken photographs. I will shortly add some examples to this review.

Undoubtedly remarkable, the iPhone 15 Pro is a smartphone that will not disappoint. It was the ideal size, in my opinion, to fit into a pocket and utilize with ease in one hand.

Specifications

Name of Product: iPhone 15 Pro;

Brand: Apple

Release Date: September 2023

Weight: 6.6 oz.

Product measurements: 2.78 by 5.77 by 0.32 inches.

The colors of titanium are natural, blue, white, and black.

Pricing begins at $999.

System: iOS 17 Processor

Apple A17 Pro Storage: 1TB (1TB tested), 256GB, 512GB, and 128GB

Primary 48MP telephoto, ultra wide, and camera system

Inputs/Outputs: USB-C

IP68 water resistance (waterproof up to 6 meters for 30 minutes)

Wonderlust's Upcoming Events: The iPhone 15's Release and Much More

Fall is almost here, which means new iPhones. We're delving into leaks, speculations, and conjecture around the iPhone 15 today.

With nearly every aspect of the iPhone Pro remaining unaltered, some fantastic new hand-me-down capabilities for the standard iPhone, and a remote chance that Apple will release an even more costly iPhone above the Pro line, this year is looking to be a vintage year for new iPhone releases. The upcoming adjustments won't spare even the charging wires.

A Fall in Unexpected Expectations

First, on Tuesday, September 12, the iPhone 15 launch event is most likely scheduled. Unless there's a holiday or some other cause to deviate, Apple typically hosts events on Tuesdays. The iPhone event typically takes place during the second full week of September.

Apple just moved the iPhone to a new product cycle. Rather of replacing the same old processors in both the Pro and normal versions annually, the new processor is now only available in the iPhone Pro, while the conventional iPhone is left with last year's model. With a new three-nanometer chip technology that uses less energy and more power, the same is anticipated this year.

As for the standard, non-Pro iPhone, don't anticipate much. It will most likely receive the incredible Dynamic Island along with improved cameras, but that may be (almost—see below) it. To be honest, it's probably sufficient.

Let's talk about USB before moving on to the iPhone Pro and potential iPhone Ultra. The iPhone 15 will support USB-C data transfer and charging instead of Lightning. You won't have to worry about as many charging cables because this complies with EU regulation, which requires

USB-C charging on all new devices.

It's expected that Apple will also make available a new USB-C cover for the AirPods and AirPods Pro.

iPhone 15 Pro

Since we've previously discussed the potent new A17 chip, let's take a brief break to discuss the cameras within the new iPhone 15 Pro. The main speculation here is that the long-awaited periscope camera—yes, exactly what it sounds like—will be included in the XL-sized iPhone Pro Max. Instead than depending on ever-larger camera bumps to cram in bigger lenses, a periscope design flips the camera on its side so it may lay along the length of the phone instead of protruding out, utilizing optics to bend the incoming light through 90 degrees.

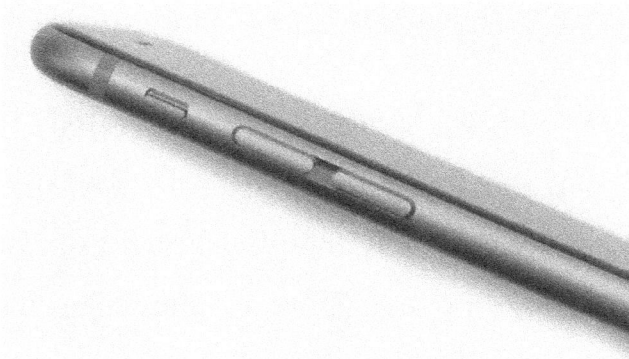

There will be much more alterations on the outside. First, since titanium is stronger, lighter, and maybe more flexible than steel, Apple may replace the steel band on the iPhone Pro. Because titanium can be anodized similarly to aluminum, additional colors for the Pro models should be anticipated. These will likely remain quite muted hues because, evidently, Pro models aren't able to appear stylish. Additionally, according to some speculations, the iPhone's back will have rounded corners to make it simpler to pocket.

And according to a [last-minute insider report], this titanium band will cut the weight of the pocket-dragging iPhone Pro model by roughly ten percent and switch to a brushed finish that won't show fingerprints like the existing smooth steel band. It's also about time, as up until now, the standard iPhone, which costs less, has an aluminum band that makes it better than the Pro model in both of these categories.

In addition, the mute switch on that titanium frame will most likely be replaced with a user-programmable action button, similar to the one seen on the Apple Watch Ultra.

I really enjoy the glanceability of the mute switch, but I also use my iPhone in silent mode almost all the time, so this one seems like a useful addition. For example, I could use it to turn on the camera and snap a picture.

Next, we have the screen itself, which will continue to be the same size yet grow larger. Of course, what we're talking about is reducing those bezels to accommodate a larger screen within the same body.

There's another reason why this year will be significant for the iPhone Pro. There have been rumors of an iPhone 15 Ultra. There's a chance that this is a completely new phone, but it could also be a rebranded version of Apple's dreadful iPhone Pro Max.

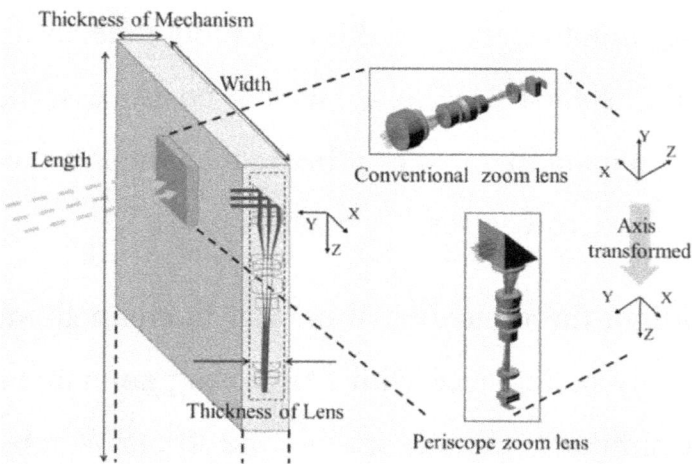

The forthcoming iOS, watchOS, and iPadOS releases will also be summarized by Apple.

In my opinion, the USB-C port on the iPhone and the periscope camera—should it ever arrive—will be the most intriguing features. Apple has been pleased with its exclusive Lighting connector and the license fees it can charge hardware manufacturers for its use for many years. It will be fascinating to watch the narrative Apple crafts to justify USB-C's superiority, all the while avoiding disparaging its own superb connector.

Even if there seem to be a lot of leaks and rumors, Apple has tightened up its privacy quite a bit in previous years, so there may be more surprises. I'll see you on September 12th!

What makes the USB-C connector on the iPhone 15 potentially significant

Some experts are happy that Apple may finally be doing away with the Lightning connector in its upcoming iPhone.

Apple is getting ready to unveil its next generation of

gadgets this fall, and rumors have it that the top-tier iPhone 15 models will have a USB-C port among other noteworthy improvements. Some claim it's past overdue to abandon Lightning.

Tech expert Mark Vena said in an email interview that "USB-C is a universal standard embraced by various manufacturers, ensuring compatibility with a wide range of devices beyond Apple products." "Also, USB-C supports faster data transfer rates and higher power delivery, allowing for quicker charging and data syncing."

Finally, USB-C?

According to Vena, consumers would benefit from an iPhone with USB-C because of its simplicity and adaptability. Because of its reversible construction, plugging is simple and orientation is not a concern. Additionally, USB-C would do away with the need for numerous cables and adapters.

"Its compatibility with various devices makes it an essential connector for modern tech enthusiasts, simplifying connectivity and enhancing the overall user experience," he stated.

In an email, The Big Phone Store's managing director, Steven Athwal, pointed out that older USB ports, such mini and micro USB, had a lot of disadvantages. According to him, the amount of power and data that could be transferred using older USB ports was restricted and they were prone to breaking.

According to Athwal, Apple's in-house Lightning connector was a more dependable, quick, and robust option for iPhones prior to the release of USB-C. He pointed out that Lightning features an 8-pin, reversible, streamlined connector that can be placed either way up.

"Since the launch of USB-C, this connector has now become an almost universal standard for Android phones in a very short space of time—and these new connectors, which can transmit even more power and data than ever before, have fully caught up to Apple's Lightning connector in almost every way," he stated.

According to Athwal, USB-C can transport data more quickly than Lightning, which has a maximum bandwidth of less than 500Mbps. In addition, it comes with standard support for fast charging up to 100W, as opposed to Apple's 20W fast charging via its Lightning connectors at the moment.

However, abandoning Lightning has certain drawbacks.

According to Athwal, Apple is anticipated to go on with its "Made for iPhone" (MFi) certification program following the move to USB-C. Apple claims that by using software to verify the authenticity of the cable, customers can be shielded from having a subpar cable break their phone.

"However, despite your other USB-C cables having exactly the same connector, you won't necessarily be able to switch between them, and it's possible that users could become confused between which of their USB-C cables is iPhone-compatible," he stated. "This could cancel out the increased cross-compatibility you get by having one universal connector type."

Vena stated that the large selection of USB-C cables available on the market, each with a different quality level, would not always deliver the anticipated charging or data transmission speeds. It's possible that the modification will require you to buy new cables and adapters.

As stated in an email interview, "the main disadvantage is that users with Lightning accessories or cables will find them incompatible without an adapter," said Jason Wise, chief editor of the gadget website EarthWeb. "This might initially lead to some inconvenience and extra costs for users who have heavily invested in Lightning devices."

Numerous Improvements for the iPhone

There will be further updates added to the iPhone 15 lineup if the reports about USB-C turn out to be true.

One claim states that the iPhone 15 and iPhone 15 Plus would sport slightly larger displays, measuring 6.12 and 6.69 inches, respectively, owing to reduced bezels. They will also include Dynamic Island design and an A16 chipset. The upcoming iPhone 15 Pro and Pro Max models will have a state-of-the-art 3nm A17 CPU, ultra-thin bezels, a titanium chassis, an upgraded battery, WiFi 6E capability, and more RAM.

"Apple typically keeps its upcoming product details confidential until the official announcement," Vena stated. On the other hand, consumers may anticipate advancements in battery life, processor speed, and camera technology based on past trends. The next iPhones may also include software innovations, 5G support, and display technology improvements that will improve user experience."

Some Reasons Your iPhone 15 Pro Probably Doesn't Need 2TB of Storage

A 2TB storage option—eight times the capacity of the entry-level MacBook Air and four times that of the base MacBook Pro—will be available with the upcoming iPhone Pro. However, it's not quite as absurd as it first appears.

The maximum storage capacity of the iPhone 15 Pro is expected to be 2TB, or two thousand gigabytes, based on insider reports. The maximum storage capacity of the current iPhone 14 Pro is 1TB, which is already far too much for most users. Even though there were no new features in the new model, this will be great news for some iPhone owners, making the upgrade worthwhile. Oh, and the iPhone now has USB-C, which is another piece of this puzzle to take into account.

"If iPhone brings USB-C and up to 2TB of storage internal, then if you were on the road and running out of space on your laptop, you could potentially transfer over a bunch of your files to your phone temporarily until you get home to clear things off," Travis Johansen, the filmmaker, said in an email. "A huge benefit of having a two terabyte phone is also just the fact that shooting 360 video in 4k or even 8K takes a ton of space."

'Reckless Abandon' on Record

For high-definition video, there is an evident requirement for additional device capacity. Modern iPhones are powerful film-making devices that can record 4K footage at up to 60 frames per second in Dolby Vision (HDR). It requires a large amount of room. So much space, in fact, if you shoot in Apple's ProRes 4K format, you cannot accomplish it on the smallest 128GB iPhone Pro. To even see the option in the settings, you need to have at least 256GB of storage.

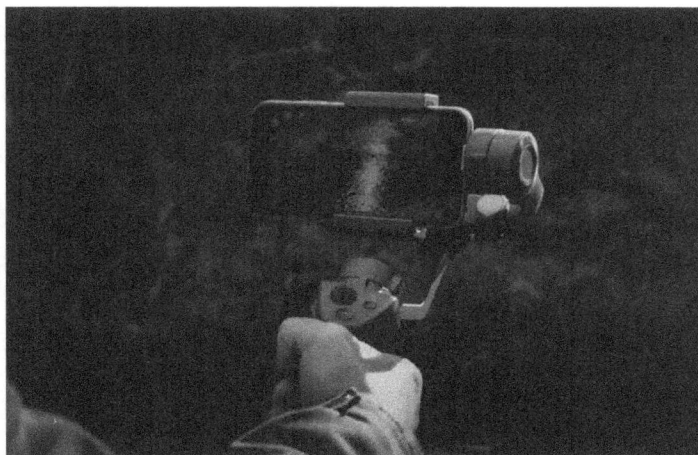

With the advancement of iPhone video capabilities, pros will be able to record TV shows and movies with just a phone. However, storage gets full quickly at that point, and since the iPhone doesn't support external storage (SD cards, for example), you need to make sure you have adequate room.

And it's not just filmmakers. Podcasters, particularly those who use video, and musicians who record numerous audio streams from various participants can also quickly fill up SSDs.

"For me, as a podcaster and content creator, I am definitely interested in the freedom of having that much space to be able to record, edit and store all of the episode assets without being tethered to the cloud," Nate Runkel, a podcaster, said in an email. The fact that I will essentially have a portable podcast studio in my pocket and be able to edit on the fly without worrying about running out of space in the middle of a project appeals to me. Additionally, it will provide me the opportunity to film 4K footage with complete abandon and without fear."

USB-C Boosts Speed of Transfer

But, in contrast to 2021, when Apple increased the storage capacity of the iPhone Pro to 1TB, there will probably be another significant shift in the way we record and store video on our iPhones—USB-C.

As required by the EU, USB-C is set to replace Lightning in the near future. Not only does this eliminate the need for you to carry an additional charging cable specifically for your iPhone, but it also has other benefits.

Lightning moves slowly. It enables USB-C-speed charging, but for data transfer, the iPhone is still limited to USB 2.0 speeds, which are capped at 480 Mbps. Compare that to the 10Gbps maximum that USB-C can support.

This implies that it's nearly hard for a photographer or videographer to get the raw material off your iPhone throughout the workday. Either you need many phones, or you need someone to help you transfer the phones while you continue shooting on a new, empty phone.

And that's before we even talk about the risks associated with not backing up your video as you go. Let's say your phone dies or gets lost and you have a day's worth of video on it.

This might be resolved with USB-C, though it's not a guarantee. The latest iPad Pro model with a Lightning connector was the 2015 edition, which could support USB 3.0 rates of up to 5Gbps. This indicates that Apple had the option to upgrade the Lightning iPhones' transfer speed at any point, but decided against it.

The 2TB iPhone 15 Pro will be a model for the pros in either case. It's true that you could save an infinite number of series, films, pictures, and videos, but why would you? You are able to stream everything. However, this is going to be fantastic news for the pros.

Arguments Against the iPhone 15 Being the Revolution You're Hoping for

It's anticipated that Apple will unveil new gadgets during its next "Wonderlust" event, but you may want to lower your expectations.

It has been reported that Apple is getting ready to release new AirPods with a USB-C charging case in place of the current Lightning port. It has also been stated that the business intends to include USB-C in upcoming iPhone models. The lackluster nature of these improvements may indicate that Apple is reaching a limit in terms of how rapidly and to what extent it can revolutionize rather than iterate its products.

Johan Alexander, CEO of APKCima, said via email that "Apple's commitment to delivering high-quality products and seamless user experiences is unquestionable." But there are certain technological constraints that the tech sector must deal with. It becomes harder to make significant advances in technology, which encourages more iterative design techniques.

Meh, Apple?

There are reports that Apple will unveil a number of goods at its event on September 12. It is reported that all versions will have 35W wireless charging. It looks that the iPhone is one of the first handsets to support the Qi2 standard, which combines wireless and magnetic charging.

The 6.7-inch screen of the suspected iPhone 15 Ultra is

anticipated to have a refresh rate of 120 Hz, thinner bezels, and a new "Action" button that would take the place of the conventional Mute button. This new button, which is a feature of the Apple Watch Ultra, is also expected to be present in the iPhone 15 Pro.

It's unlikely that the Apple Watches of this year—especially the Series 9—will alter all that much. They will probably receive minor speed and battery life improvements, though. New health features might also be implemented. In addition, a fresh shade of pink might be added for the next series.

While useful, USB-C on iPhones and other devices is hardly the stuff of tech fantasies. It is accurate to say that Apple has promised to release the revolutionary Vision Pro headset. But, the headset won't be available until the following year, and at $3500, it will be beyond the budget of many people.

Has Apple lost its magic, then?

Tech expert Arun Dhanaraj wrote in an email, "One possibility is that expectations for Apple's innovation and groundbreaking features have been set so high that anything less might be seen as underwhelming." "Additionally, leaks or speculations about the products may have dampened the element of surprise, leading to a lukewarm response from enthusiasts."

According to Alexander, Apple's need on cutting-edge parts, such as the newest CPUs, to power iPhones, can also cause problems with supply chain availability.

"Balancing the aesthetics and functionality for which Apple is known can sometimes restrict radical design changes," he stated. "Additionally, regulatory constraints can limit innovation in specific areas, such as privacy and security."

Tech expert Mark Vena said in an email that as the smartphone market has grown, it is becoming more challenging to deliver revolutionary innovations with every new edition of the iPhone. "Phone design has reached a point where further enhancements, such as camera improvements or faster processors, can only go so far in driving consumer excitement," he stated. "This limitation is not unique to Apple but affects the entire industry."

Ways Apple Can Continue To Develop

According to Alexander, Apple must make even greater investments in R&D to find or develop novel technologies that have the potential to completely redefine product categories if it is to continue producing innovative products.

"Enhancing the integration between hardware and software is essential to creating more cohesive user experiences," he stated. "Prioritizing sustainability initiatives is becoming increasingly important in addressing environmental concerns."

Vena pointed out that Apple needs to go beyond simply offering incremental hardware updates like connectors or charging standards. He claimed that the corporation may differentiate itself by emphasizing ecosystem integration, user experience improvements, and software breakthroughs.

"Investing in augmented reality (AR), artificial intelligence (AI), and sustainable technologies are areas where Apple can push boundaries," he stated. "Additionally, exploring new product categories or revolutionary form factors could rejuvenate their product lineup."

According to Mac Steer, the creator of the software startup Simify, Apple must likewise innovate its user experience.

"The first time I used an Apple product, it was so intuitive, it felt like I was using something that had been made for me personally," he stated. "It's a shame that they've lost that feeling as they've grown more generic."

The iPhone 15 Pro's Action Button Has Nine Uses.

The iPhone 15 Pro and Pro Max feature a new button called Action. On earlier iterations as well as the 15 and 15 Plus, it takes the place of the Silent Mode option. You can turn on shortcuts, open programs, and turn off your phone. This is all that you can accomplish.

1 *Start the Silent Mode (Default)*

As with the preceding switch, silent mode is the default setting. Long-press the Action button to use it in its current state. (The button located above the volume controls on the left side of the phone.)

Go to Settings > Action Button and choose an option from the list below to personalize the Action button.

2. *Turn on the camera*

utilize the Action button as a shortcut if you need to utilize the camera more quickly than you can click the app icon. Ideal for taking pictures at a party or when traveling.

3. Select an Accessibility Option

Have a preferred accessibility feature? This button can be used as a shortcut for features like Live Captions, VoiceOver (a screen reader), and color inversion.

4. Record a Voice Note

When conducting fieldwork, research, or any other task requiring you to take quick notes without forgetting anything, having a shortcut to launch a voice memo is invaluable.

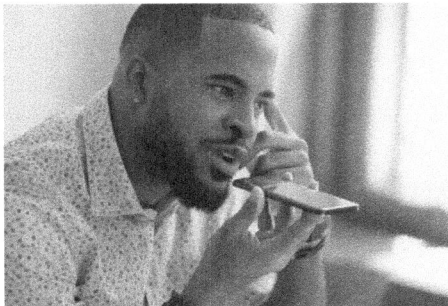

5. Start a Quick Cut

Rather than interacting with a Widget or asking Siri, you can use the Action Button to carry out your preferred Shortcut.

For iOS devices, Shortcuts is a free program that you can configure to perform various things, such calculating tips, playing a playlist, finding the travel time to a location without using a navigation tool, and much more.

6. Switch on the torch

Going camping? during a performance held outdoors? Are you having trouble navigating a strange place? With a quick (long) button press, get light. Press it once again to switch it off.

7. Select the Focus Mode

Use the button to turn on and off Focus Mode if you catch yourself daydreaming or fiddling with your phone instead of working on your task. Focus Mode is similar to Do Not Disturb, except it lets you make automatic replies and customize call, message, and notification filters.

8. Open the Magnifier Application

Use the Magnifier app to give yourself a magnifying glass.

9. Interpret a Discussion

This is a terrific idea if you're traveling or interacting with individuals from different languages so you can translate quickly.

Chapter 3

Your iPhone 15 Isn't Making Sound? Try These 12 Fixes

Once you don't hear any kind of sound on your iPhone 15, there are many actions you can take to repair the problem. The problem may be common from your iPhone, or it could only be a problem that occurs in a single app.

The key reason why your iPhone isn't making noise will probably reveal itself using the corresponding fix. Adhere to these steps in the buyer's manual to get your iPhone working once again.

<u>Check the iPhone speaker.</u> Select Configurations > Seems & Haptics. Under Ringers and Notifications, shift the slider to the proper to increase the quantity. If you can hear any sort of audio or sound, This indicates that the iPhone loudspeaker works. Until you hear audio or sound, the device might need a hardware restoration. Contact Apple Assistance.

Change the Ring/Silent switch. The Ring/Silent change, also known as the Mute change, has two jobs. When the change is forced toward the trunk of these devices, the color orange seems to indicate that this change is defined as a silent setting. Push the change toward the display to enable audio.

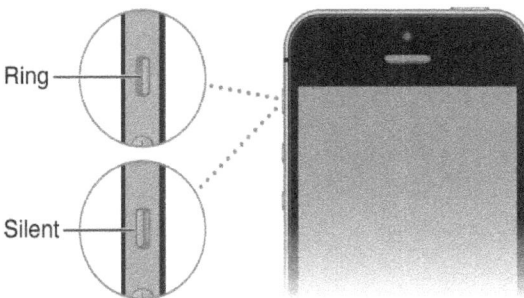

Ring

Silent

Turn off Do Not Disturb. *Usually, Do Not Disturb* setting silences many noises and alerts. Turn it off unless you hear any audio. Open the Configurations app, select *Usually Do Not Disturb*, then shift the toggle change to the Off placement.

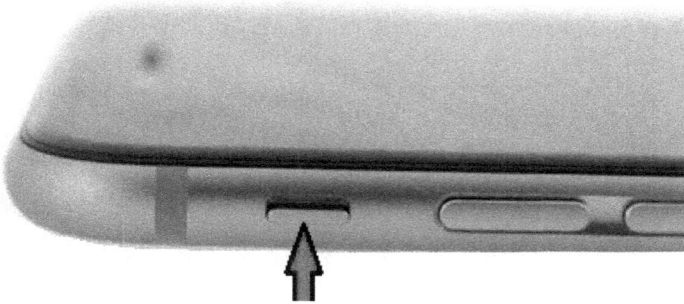

Disable Bluetooth. Whenever your iPhone will be linked to a Bluetooth sound device, it transmits sound to these devices and not to the speaker on the iPhone. Switch off Bluetooth, so that noises play from your iPhone.

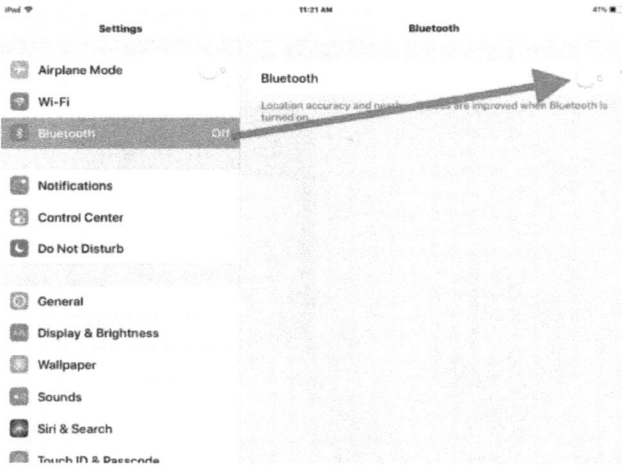

Adjust the volume buttons in an app. Occasionally the sound volume in an app could be turned down as well as low to listen to. Open up an app, such as Songs, Podcasts, or any app that utilizes sound. Utilize the volume buttons privately from the iPhone to carefully turn up the quantity.

It may furthermore be the sound setting in the app that is too low. Open up the app and demand page using the Have fun with/Pause button. Proceed the slider to the proper to increase the volume.

Examine third-party app audio settings. Numerous third-party apps offer you customized quantity and mute audio settings. For instance, some games present separate configurations for music, sound files, ambient audio, and much more.

In the app, search for audio or sound settings. Switch off any personalized mute options, allow audio, and change the button sliders to increase volume. With regards to the app, either shift sliders up, shift sliders to the proper, or faucet an icon to create it active.

Check notification configurations for the app. Examine the iPhone notifications' audio settings for your app. Some apps, such as Reminders and Communications, allow you to select notification audio. If this audio is defined to none, the alert will be silent. Tap none and select audio.

Try headsets. Find the earphones that were included with the iPhone. For old iPhone versions, plug the headsets into the headset slot. For newer iPhone versions, plug the headphone into the Lightning interface. (The charging wire also connects to this slot.) Pay attention to sound with the earphones while making use of an app that provides audio.

Restart these devices. If you nevertheless don't hear any audio, restart the iPhone. To restart, turn the iPhone off and back on.

Look for app updates. In rare circumstances, having less sound will be the consequence of an app creator error. Head to App Shop > Updates to check on if an app update is available.

Check for program updates. An iOS update might fix an audio problem. Look for any system software updates from Apple, then download and install the available updates.

Reset all settings. If none of the aforementioned steps handle your sound problem, reset the iPhone configurations. This resets the audio, display, and system settings towards the iPhone defaults. Head to Configurations > Common > Reset > Reset All Configurations.

Can't Download Apps on iPhone 15? 11 Ways to Make It Better

It could be incredibly frustrating whenever your iPhone won't download apps. In the end, applications are part of the actual iPhone, so excellent. No matter whether you're aiming to download new applications or update applications you currently have, you want this to work. Fortunately, fixing this issue is not too difficult.

What Prevents iPhone Apps From Installing?

While mending an iPhone that won't download applications is not too difficult, what can cause the problem isn't quite so simple. Actually, there are almost as much potential factors behind this mistake as there are fixes for this. These range between App Store guidelines to simple insects, from issues with your Apple ID to your iPhone's configurations and more. Instead of providing a summary of the causes here, each solution below provides some history for the problem.

How to Fix an iPhone That Isn't Allowing App Downloads

If applications won't download to your iPhone, try these fixes, in this order.

- Try Wi-Fi. If you are aiming to download the application more than a mobile connection like 4G LTE, you may be hitting a restriction of the App Store. Apple limitations how big is app downloading over mobile to 150 MB. That is done to avoid users from using too much data about the same download. If the application you want to download is bigger than that, hook up to Wi-Fi. It is also smart to check to ensure you are not in Airplane Setting, which blocks all Wi-Fi and mobile network connections.

- Restart the App Store app. The insect in installing the app may need to do with the App Store application itself. If something will go wrong with this app, it will not have the ability to help set up the application you want. If so, restarting the App Store application may clear the insect. Then, just re-open the App Store application and make an effort to re-download the app.

- Pause and restart the application download. This suggestion only works on devices with a 3D Touchscreen (the iPhone 6S and newer, aside from the iPhone XR). It works whenever your application download has been interfered with for reasons unknown. If an application icon shows up on your home display, however the download seems sluggish or like it isn't occurring, hard press the icon for the application you're trying to set up. In the menu that pops right out of the icon, faucet Resume Download (whether it's already paused). You can do the same thing in the App Store app, on the display screen for the application you want to set up.

- Restart iPhone. Exactly like restarting the App Store application can solve the issue of apps not installing on your iPhone, sometimes you will need to restart all of your phone. This may be because the short-term glitch in your telephone could maintain the operating-system or another area of the phone's software. A restart will most likely resolve that type of issue.

- Check your Apple ID payment methods. To be able to download apps, you must have a payment method on document in your Apple ID. That is true even if you are aiming to download a free of charge app. So, unless you have a payment method on document, or if you have a card that's expired, you will possibly not have the ability to download apps.

This may also business lead to a Confirmation Required pop-up message. Get yourself a valid payment method on document and you may be able to begin downloading applications again.

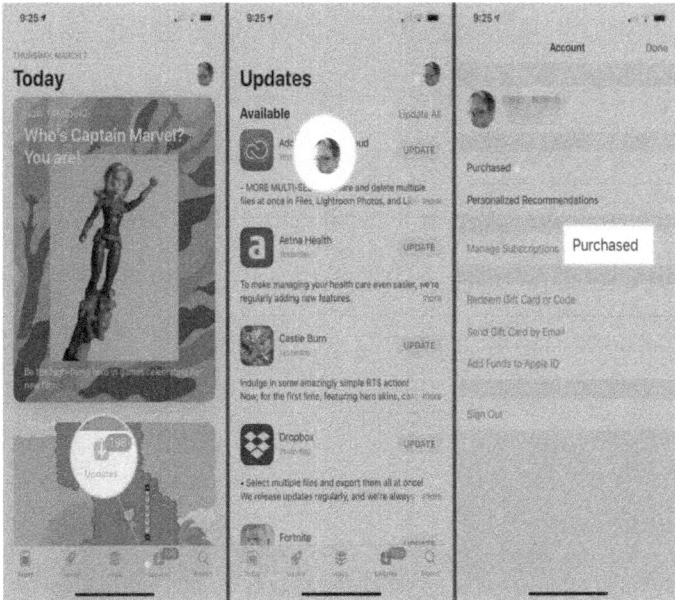

- Sign from the App Store and indication back. An iPhone that can't download applications may be considered an indication that something is up with your Apple ID. If the bond created by your Apple ID in the middle of your iPhone and the App Store gets disrupted, sometimes simply putting your signature on out and putting your signature on back will correct it. To achieve that, touch

Configurations > iTunes & App Store > Apple ID > Indication Out. Then, indication back by tapping *Register* and getting into your Apple ID account.

- Upgrade iOS. Whenever Apple produces an upgrade to the iOS - the operating-system that works on the iPhone, iPad, and iPod itouch - the new software fixes pests. Maybe your iPhone can't download applications due to an insect in the operating-system. A straightforward, fast, and free Operating-system revise may solve your trouble.

- Set correct day and time. Contrary to popular belief, but the time and time configurations on your mobile phone being incorrect can stop you from downloading apps. The simplest way to resolve this is to make your iPhone automatically arranged its day and time so that it is always correct. To achieve that, tap Configurations > General > Day & Time > move the Arranged Automatically slider on/green.

- Reset iPhone device configurations. Bugs like applications not installing on your iPhone can often be the effect of a small problem in your low-level configurations. You can't always see these configurations or fix them separately, however the iOS provides you ways to reset all configurations. Accomplishing this won't erase your computer data, but can solve these kinds of issues.

- Check the Apple ID you're using. If you are creating a problem upgrading an application already on your device, the problem may be the Apple ID you're using. When you download an app, it's linked with the Apple ID you're logged into at that time. In the event that you change the Apple ID you're using, applications linked with the old ID will not be able to upgrade. Try putting your signature on into other Apple IDs you've used, following an instruction in step 7 above.

- Get help from Apple. If you have tried many of

these steps as well as your iPhone still won't download apps, you will need help from professionals at Apple. You may get online or telephone support via Apple's website or you may make a scheduled appointment at the Genius Pub at your neighborhood Apple Store for in-person help.

What To Do If Your iPhone 15 Isn't Updating Apps

Ever come across a situation where your iPhone can't update apps? It's uncommon, but it may also be a pretty complicated situation, especially because upgrading applications on your iPhone is usually as easy as tapping a few buttons. There are a lot of ways to resolve this problem, however the fixes aren't apparent. In case your iPhone won't upgrade apps and you understand your web connection is working fine (because you can't download applications without that!), I'm assuring you that you're reading the right book for the solution. This book has methods for getting your iPhone upgrading apps again.

1 Restart iPhone

A straightforward step that can solve many iPhone problems is restarting these devices. Sometimes your mobile phone just must be reset. When it begins fresh, things that didn't work before instantly do, including upgrading apps. To restart your iPhone:

- Keep down the rest/wake (or Part) button.
- When the slider shows up near the top of the display screen, move it from remaining to right.
- Allow iPhone switch off.
- If it is off, keep down the rest/wake button again before Apple logo shows up.
- Forget about the button and allow phone set up as normal.

2 Pause and Restart the App Download

A problem downloading an application may also be caused by the bond between your telephone and the App Store getting interrupted. You are able to reset that connection by pausing the download and restarting it. This program is a little concealed, but here's where to find it:

- Find the icon your "home screen" for the application that you're wanting to download.
- Tap and keep it (on devices with 3D Touch displays, press hard onto it).

- In the menu that pops out, faucet Pause Download.

- Wait an instant, then touch the application icon again to resume the download.

3 Update to the most recent Version of iOS

Another common solution to numerous problems is to ensure you're operating the latest version of the iOS. That is especially important when you can't revise apps, since improvements to apps may need a more recent version of the iOS than you have.

Methods for Wirelessly Editing iOS on an iPhone

Each new version of iOS-the operating-system that runs the iPhone-brings new features, bug fixes, and changes from what the telephone can do and exactly how it's used. Improving to a fresh version of iOS used to involve linking the iOS device to a Personal computer, downloading the upgrade to the computer, then setting up the revise by syncing with iTunes. Nowadays, iOS improvements can be installed wirelessly (a method known as over-the-air, or OTA, upgrading).

The Best Way to Update iOS on an iPhone Wirelessly

Before you start an update:

- Back up your computer data to iCloud or iTunes should in case something goes wrongly with the update and the telephone must be restored.

- Hook up to a Wi-Fi network. The upgrade can be downloaded more than a mobile network; however, the improvements are large (often 1GB or even more), might take quite a while to download, and use your regular monthly cellular data. Wi-Fi is simpler and faster.

- Charge the iPhone electric battery. The download and set up process does take time. If there's significantly less than 50 percent electric battery life staying, charge the electric battery before the revise.

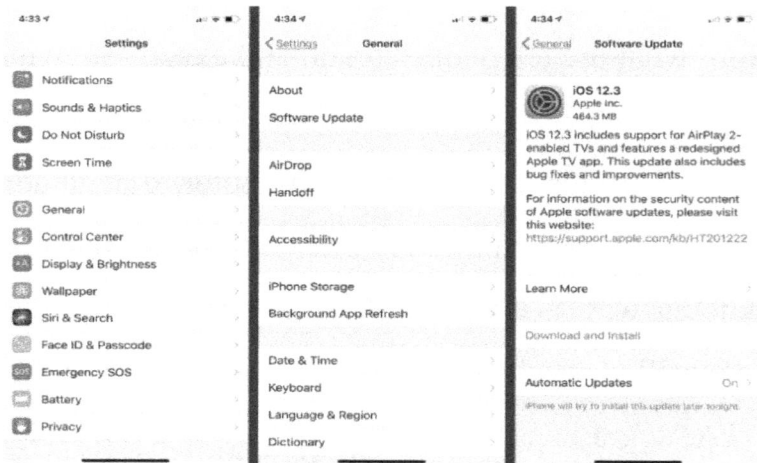

To upgrade iOS:

- For the iPhone Home display, tap the Configurations app.

- Scroll down, then faucet General.

- Tap Software Revise. The device investigations to find out if there's a revise. When there is, it reviews what it is and the actual upgrade increases the device.

- Touch Download and Install to start setting up the iPhone software revise.

- If the telephone is shielded with a passcode, enter the passcode to start the download. A blue improvement bar moves over the screen.

- Touch Install Now. The display screen will go dark, then shows the Apple logo. An improvement pub shows the position of the upgrade. When the iOS revise coatings, the iPhone restarts and shows a conclusion notice.

Tricks for iOS Upgrade

The iPhone notifies you when there's an update even though you don't look for it. If you visit a red 1 icon the

Configurations application on your home display, which means there's an iOS upgrade available. You may even receive a force notification.

If there is not enough empty space for storage available on these devices to set up the update, understand how to update iPhone when you do not have enough space and follow the tips to repair this situation.

If something goes wrongly with the installation, there are two options to repair it: Recovery Setting or (if things go badly) DFU Setting. Another consequence of a failed update is a white display screen of death.

How To Get The Latest iOS Updates And Install Them

When Apple produces a fresh update to iOS - the operating-system that works the iPhone, iPod itouch, and iPad - set it up. Updates to iOS deliver insect fixes, user interface tweaks, and new features. Update to the latest version of the iOS in two ways: through iTunes or on the iPhone. To revise on the iPhone, see how to upgrade iOS wirelessly on the iPhone. Here's how to execute the revise using iTunes on macOS and Home windows computers.

How to Upgrade iOS Using iTunes

Using iTunes to upgrade your iPhone or iPad is an excellent option if your iOS device is low on space. Follow these steps to keep the device current even whether it's full.

- Connect the iOS device to the computer you sync it with and release iTunes.

- Click on the icon for your device to open up these devices' management screen.

- Click Sync or **Backup** Now to either sync these devices with the computer or produce a back-up of the info on the telephone. It's good to truly have a back-up in the event anything goes incorrect with the upgrade.

- Click Sync or **Support** Now to either sync these devices with the computer or develop a back-up of the info on the telephone. It's good to truly have a back-up should in case anything goes wrong with the update.

- When the sync is complete, the iPhone management display shows the version of iOS on these devices and information in regards to a newer version if the first is available. Click Revise to start the process.

- Click Download And then download the program for a later revise or click Download and Install to upgrade now.

- Browse the information about new features, fixes, and changes the new version of the iOS offers, then click Next.

- Click Consent to acknowledge an individual agreement.

- The revise downloads and automatically installs on your device. If prompted, follow the instructions.

- When the set-up is complete, these devices will automatically restart.

4 Ensure that You're Using the appropriate Apple ID

If you cannot update apps, start by confirming if you are using the right Apple ID. When you download an app, it's linked with the Apple ID you used when you downloaded it. Which means that you'll require to be logged into that original Apple ID to use the application on your iPhone. On your own iPhone, check what Apple ID was used to get an application by following these steps:

- Touch the App Store app.
- Tap Updates.
- Touch your picture or icon in the very best right part (skip this task in iOS 10 or previously).
- Tap Purchased.
- Determine if the application is right here. If not, it was likely downloaded with another Apple ID.

If you are using iTunes (and are owning a version that still shows your apps; iTunes 12.7 removed the App Store and apps), you can confirm what Apple ID was used to get an application by following these steps:

- Head to your set of apps.
- Right-click the application you have in mind.
- Click Get Info.
- Click the Document tab.
- Take a look at Purchased by for the Apple ID.

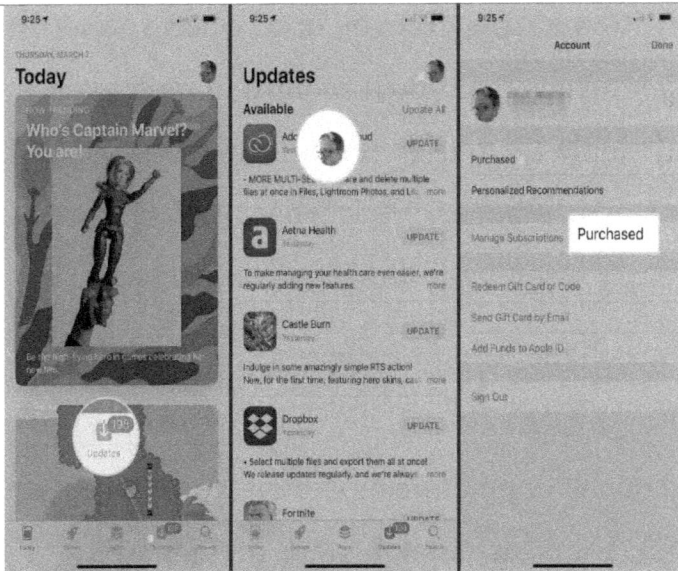

If you used another Apple ID before, try logging into that person's account to find out if it fixes your problem (Settings -> iTunes & App Stores -> Apple ID).

5 Ensure Restrictions Are Off

The Limitations feature of the iOS is, by iOS 12, situated in the Display Time settings. It enables people (usually parents or corporate and business IT administrators) disable certain top features of the iPhone. One particular feature is the capability to download apps. So, if you cannot install an upgrade, the feature may be blocked.

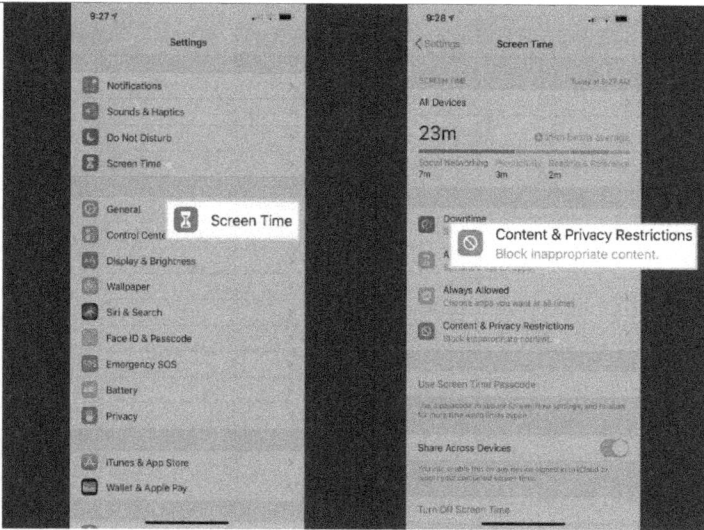

To check on this or switch off app limitations, follow these steps:

- Tap Settings.

- Tap Display screen Time.

- Touch Content & Personal privacy Restrictions.

- Tap Content Limitations.

- Tap Apps. Be certain that All Apps is examined.

In previous versions of the iOS, Restrictions are positioned in Settings -> General -> Restrictions.

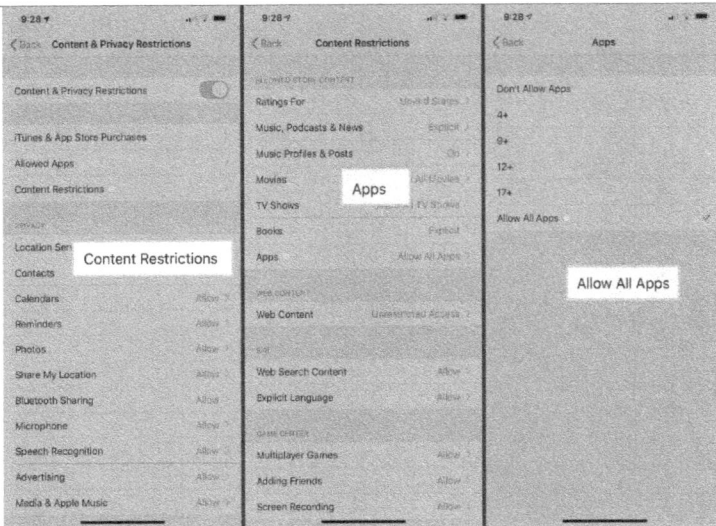

6 Sign Out And Back To The App Store

Sometimes, all you have to do to repair an iPhone that can't revise applications is to sign in and out of your Apple ID. It's simple, but that can solve the problem. Some tips about what you must do:

- Tap Settings.
- Touch iTunes & App Store.
- Touch the Apple ID menu (it lists the e-mail address you utilize for your Apple ID).
- In the pop-up menu, faucet Sign Out.
- Touch the Apple ID menu again and register with your Apple ID.

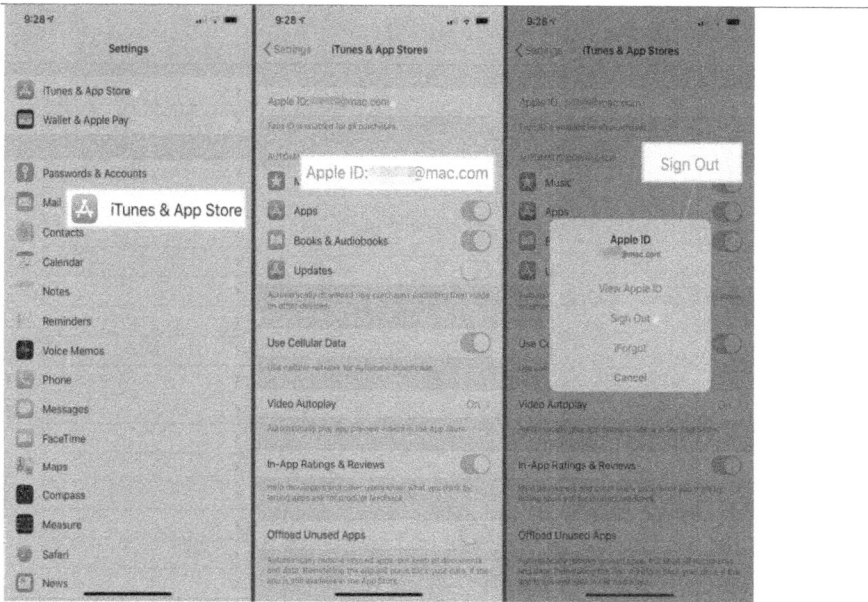

7 Check Available Storage

Here is a simple description: Perhaps you can't install the application update because you do not have enough available space for storage on your iPhone. If you very, hardly any free storage, the telephone might not have the area it requires to execute the upgrade and easily fit into the new version of the app.

Check your free space for storage by pursuing these steps:

- Tap Settings.
- Tap General.
- Tap About.
- Search for the Available collection. That's how

much free space you have.

In case your available storage space is surprisingly low, try deleting some data that's not necessary like apps, photos, podcasts, or videos.

8. Change Day and Time Setting

Your iPhone's day and time settings influence whether it can update apps. The reason why because of this are complicated, but essentially, your iPhone performs lots of inspections when interacting with Apple's servers to do things such as update apps. One particular check is perfect for time. In case your configurations are wrong, it can prevent you from having the ability to update apps.

To solve this issue, set your day and time for you to automatically update your apps by following these steps:

- Tap Settings.
- Tap General.
- Tap Time & Time.
- Move the Arranged Automatically slider to on/green.

9 Delete and Reinstall the App

If nothing at all else spent some time working up to now, try deleting and reinstalling the app. Sometimes an application just requires a fresh start so when you do that, you'll install the latest version of the app.

10 Reset All Settings

Should in case you still can't update apps, you may want to try slightly more drastic steps to get things working again. The first option here's to try resetting your iPhone's configurations.

This won't delete any data from your phone. It just reverts a few of your requirements and settings with their original says. You can transform them back again after your applications are upgrading again. Here's how to do it:

- Tap Settings.

- Tap General.

- Tap Reset.

- Touch Reset All Configurations.

- You might be asked to enter your passcode. If you're, do so.

- In the pop-up windows, touch Reset All Configurations.

11 Update the App Using iTunes

If an application won't update on your iPhone, try carrying it out through iTunes (assuming you utilize iTunes with your telephone). Upgrading this way is fairly simple:

- On your pc, launch iTunes.
- Select Apps from the drop-down menu at the very top left.
- Click Updates underneath the top windowpane.
- Single-click the icon of the application you want to revise.
- In the section that starts, click the Upgrade button.
- When the application has up to date, sync your iPhone like normal and install the up to date app.

12 Bring back iPhone to Factory Settings

Lastly, if absolutely nothing else spent some time working, it is time to try the most drastic step of most: deleting from your iPhone and configuring it from scratch. This is a larger process, so we have a complete article specialized in this issue: How exactly to Restore iPhone to Factory Configurations.

After that's done, you may even want to revive your iPhone from backup.

How to Fix an Effective iPhone Bug

Strategies for resolving normal iPhone problems. The

iPhone will be the hottest smartphone, nonetheless, it is in no way perfect. A lot of customers report annoying display glitches along with other issues with no obvious cause. In case your iPhone is glitching, follow these pointers to recognize and repair the problem.

Glitches can be found in all sizes and shapes, and for you to repair this depends on the sort of glitch you're experiencing. Many problems have their very own set of possible solutions. Adhere to these troubleshooting suggestions, in order, to get your iPhone operating again.

Quit or close up issue apps. iOS occasionally crashes or leads to a variety of issues, but force-closing and relaunching apps frequently solve those difficulties.

Restart the iPhone. Restarting your iPhone can resolve a bunch of problems, which includes a frozen display screen. The guidelines for restarting an iPhone can be determined by your particular design.

Hold Home Button

Hold Power Button

Update iOS. Frequently upgrading an iPhone may be the most effective device to avoid glitches. Often, Apple company consists of fixes for recognized glitches that may be used by installing the brand new edition of iOS.

Register and from the Apple ID. A typical error is once the App Shop continuously refreshes but in no way loads. The ultimate way to stop this is to restart the phone. If it doesn't work, register and from the Apple Identification. *Select Configurations > iTunes & App Shop > Apple Identification,* then select Indication Out. Following that, use the same process to indicate back in.

Disable background refresh for apps you do not use or don't need to have. Even though you don't open up apps, numerous apps refresh in the backdrop, which may place pressure on the mobile phone and its electric battery, especially if you utilize information or processing-intensive apps. Head to *Configurations* > *Common* > *History App Refresh.* It is possible to disable history refresh for several apps or go for ones.

Disable automated updates. Apps that don't operate in the backdrop download updates instantly, and if there are lots of updates, it could slow down the phone. To shut this down, choose *Configurations* > *iTunes & App Shop.* Under Auto Downloads, toggle App Up-dates to off. You can even turn off automated updates for Songs, Apps, and Publications & Audiobooks.

Crystal clear the Safari cache. Every internet browser collects data as time passes to help it better to navigate the web. While hassle-free, the cache can sluggish a tool when it gets too big. To delete the cache, head to Configurations > Safari > Crystal clear History and Web site Data, then concur that you want to delete the info.

Look for iOS up-date and restore mistakes. Some glitches prevent you from upgrading iOS, which leads to error rules. While short and fairly cryptic, these rules show you the issue that prevents you from upgrading or restoring these devices. Consult Apple's set of upgrade and restore mistakes to get your error, after that follow the training to repair it.

Apple Pay might stop downloads until it is updated. If Apple Pay doesn't revise, take your phone into an Apple company store.

If you get an alert stating, *"Cellular Update Failed,"* this can be an issue using the phone's cellular modem. Go to an Apple company Shop or Genius Pub to repair it.

Try various Wi-Fi networks. If you are at work, college, or any other area where you register for the Wi-Fi every time you enter, this might interfere with Apple company up-dates. Use a general public Wi-Fi link or disable Wi-Fi if the app improves using a mobile connection. Head to Configurations > Wi-Fi, after that faucet the Wi-Fi toggle to disable Wi-Fi. Afterward, either discover and hook up to a new system or wait just a few minutes to reconnect to your present network.

Reset the system settings. When you have issues with Wi-Fi or mobile information, reset the system settings. You can even instruct these devices to forget a particular network, which causes the iPhone to disconnect from your network.

Reset the router. Restart your products in a string to diagnose the issue. At first, restart the iPhone. When the system problem persists, restart the Wi-Fi router, then your modem. If none of these solves the problem, there is most likely an outage together with your internet service supplier, and there is nothing you can do but wait.

Clear iCloud storage space or buy even more. In case your iPhone doesn't back up on iCloud, first, check out your storage configurations. Go to Configurations, select your title, then go for iCloud > Manage Storage space. In case your iCloud will be complete, download an iCloud power app to your personal computer and utilize it to download and backup files you no longer need immediate access to, such as old photos. Producing some space can solve several problems, or you can purchase more areas from Apple.

Clear the iPhone. Some gadgets, particularly old types, create hardware troubles as dirt and residue build-up. It is possible to clear, sanitize, and disinfect the phone but take care not to trigger damage along the way.

Troubleshoot the camera. In case your iPhone's digital camera is around the fritz, open up the App of the Digital camera and touch the flip symbol in the lower-right part to find out if both front side and back digital cameras are unavailable. Only if the rear digital camera is affected, take away the iPhone case and find out if it solves the problem. Some iPhones are not made with the rear digital camera in mind. Only when the front digital camera is affected, switch the phone off and cautiously clean the leading of the telephone with a dried out fabric. If both aren't working, restart these devices. If that's inadequate, there is most likely a hardware issue, and you'll have to get the iPhone for an Apple Store.

Protect your iPhone data. Hackers may try to hack, freeze, or sometimes glitch your iPhone, and the ultimate way to keep them out would be to protect your computer data and exercise safe conduct online. Don't open email messages or attachments on your phone if you are uncertain who sent the communications. The same will additionally apply to texts. Don't open texts from numbers you do not know.

Confirm that the thing is not hardware-related. The collection between a software program problem along a hardware concern can be slim. The simplest way to confirm it is not a software problem, or at the very least, not one it is possible to resolve, would be to inspect these devices for physical harm. Look for splits or distortions in the casing. If you discover any sign of physical harm impairing the telephone, go on to Apple company for repairs.

Get the iPhone from an Apple company Store. If none of the aforementioned tips resolved the issue, give the iPhone to some repair specialist or Apple company Genius Bar.

Try various Wi-Fi networks. If you are at work, college, or any other place where you register for the Wi-Fi each time you enter, this might interfere with Apple company up-dates. Use an open public Wi-Fi link or disable Wi-Fi if the app improves when using a mobile connection. Head to Configurations > Wi-Fi, after that faucet the Wi-Fi toggle to disable Wi-Fi. Afterward, either discover and hook up to a new system or wait just a few minutes to reconnect to your present network.

Make your iPhone do the job. The iPhone packages a huge amount of great features, nevertheless, you can make it even more effective by unlocking the iPhone hacks and methods hiding in your smartphone. You can find a huge selection of these key features, but listed below are our picks for that 15 greatest iPhone hacks.

01 Cost Your Electric battery Faster

Want to cost your iPhone's electric battery as fast as possible? Place it in Aircraft Mode first. Aircraft Mode tends off many top features of the phone, which includes mobile and Wi-Fi social networking, so there's much less for your battery to accomplish and it costs faster. Remember to turn Aircraft Mode off if you are done charging.

To use Aircraft Mode: Open Handle Middle (swipe down from the very best directly on iPhone X or more or upward from underneath on other choices) and faucet the aircraft icon.

Notice: This hack functions on all iPhone versions.

02 Shutting Apps Doesn't Save Electric battery Life

You might have heard that quitting apps helps your iPhone battery last longer. Regardless of how many individuals state it, it's not true. Quitting apps can make your electric battery require a recharge faster. So, don't stop apps you are not using-just keep them in the backdrop.

Take note: This hack functions on all iPhone versions.

03 Discover the Strongest Nearby Cellular Signal

Talk about a concealed feature! Neglect waving your mobile phone in the airflow and traveling to get the most powerful cellular signal. Simply use this technique and you'll get yourself a clear indicator of signal power:

- Open the telephone app.

- Dial *3001#12345#*.

- Tap the decision button.

- In iOS 6 through 10, this loads the Field Test display and you may skip to step 7. On iOS 11 or more, it loads the Primary Menu.

- Tap LTE.

- Tap Serving Cellular Meas to check out the ranges rsrp0 (your present cellular tower) and rsrp1 (the closest back-up tower).

- Tap the transmission strength indication in the very

best left corner.

The lower the quantity, the higher the signal. Therefore - 90 is a superb sign, -110 will be OK, and -125 is not good indication at all. Stroll around to observe how the transmission strength modifications and make use of your cell phone where you've got a low number.

Be aware: This hack functions on iPhones operating iOS 6 through iOS 10. On mobile phones working on iOS 11, your phone will need an Intel modem in it. Models that will be the iPhone 12, iPhone 11 and 11 Pro, iPhone XS, iPhone XR, iPhone X: (A1901), iPhone 8: (A1905), iPhone 8 Plus: (A1897), iPhone 7: (A1778), and iPhone 7 Plus: (A1784).

04 Create a Lighting Blink like a Notification

Need to get notifications of fresh texts, incoming phone calls, or some other useful info without looking at your iPhone display screen or hearing sounds? With this particular hack, the digital camera flash on the trunk of the phone blinks when you have a fresh notification. Just adhere to these actions:

- Tap Settings.

- Tap Common (skip this task on iOS 13 or more).

- Tap Accessibility.

- Tap Sound/Visual (neglect this step about iOS 13 or more).

- Tap LED Adobe to flash for Notifications (skip this task in iOS 13 or more).

- Proceed the slider to on. Also shift the Display on Silent slider to on.

Notice: This hack functions on all iPhone versions with a digital camera flash.

05 Take Photos With the Volume Button

Did you know that tapping the on-screen camera button isn't the only path to take pictures? There's an easier way to get photos rapidly, without considering or tapping the display. Once the Digital camera app is open, click on the volume up switch, and your mobile phone snaps a photo. This even works with headphones that have inline remotes.

Take note: *This hack functions on all iPhone versions.*

Some models may take pictures with the button down, too.

06 Allow Siri To Help You To Take Photos

Everyone knows they can ask Siri queries but do you realize Siri could help you get photos faster? Although it can't capture the photo, Siri can open the Camera app towards the setting that you require, so you simply need to tap the camera button (or click on the volume button). Some tips about what to accomplish:

Activate Siri (hold straight down the house or Part button, based on your magic size) and have Siri to have a photo or video. Your alternatives are:

- "Hey Siri, have a picture" (you can even say "image")

- "Hey Siri, have a square picture"

- "Hey Siri, have a panoramic photograph"

- "Hey Siri, have a video"

- "Hey Siri, have a slow-motion movie"

- "Hey Siri, have a tap-lapse movie"

- "Hey Siri, have a selfie."

Once you have the image you need, touch the camera or volume button.

Be aware: This hack functions on all iPhone versions. The selfie function needs iOS 10 or more.

07 Type Your Orders to Siri Rather than Speaking Them

Siri is fantastic, nevertheless, you can't talk with Siri and obtain answers aloud in every scenario (and, for a lot of people with disabilities, speaking may not be a choice). In those cases, you should use Siri if you'll have Typed to Siri fired up. This trick enables you to access Siri and present it commands by typing. Some tips about what to accomplish:

- Tap Settings.

- Tap Common (skip this task on iOS 13 or more).

- Tap Accessibility.

- Tap Siri.

- Move the sort to Siri slider to on/environment friendly.

Right now, activate Siri, along with a keyboard seems to

let you know your command. You can even speak utilizing the microphone icon.

Notice: This hack works on all iPhone models running iOS 11 or more.

08 Work with a Hidden Dark Mode

HINT: Using the launch of iOS 13, the official Black Mode continues to be put into the iPhone. Learn to utilize it by reading through How to Enable Black Setting on iPhone and iPad.

Dark modes certainly are a popular function for those who often make use of their devices at night. With the dark setting enabled, your iPhone user interface switches to darkish colors which are easier for the eye in low-light circumstances (they're also ideal for people with color blindness). As the iPhone doesn't provide a correct dark setting, this trick will get you petty near:

- Tap Settings.

- Tap General.

- Tap Accessibility.

- Tap Display Lodging.

- Tap Invert Colours.

- Pick either Wise Invert (which switches some on-screen colors to Dark Setting) or Vintage Invert (which switches all shades).

- It is possible to toggle the dark mode on / off easily.

Take note: This hack functions on all iPhone versions operating iOS 11 or more.

09 Put in a Virtual House Button for your Screen

When you have an iPhone X or newer version just iPhone 12, you may skip the old hardware Home key. Even though you possess another model, you may want your options and features to include a virtual House switch for your screen. This can be an excellent hack since it offers quick access to functions that otherwise need gestures or several taps. Make it possible for this virtual House key:

- Tap Settings.

- Tap Common (skip this task on iOS 13 or more).

- Tap Accessibility.

- Faucet Touch (just do this about iOS 13 or more).

- Tap AssistiveTouch.

- Shift the slider to on/natural.

Be aware: This hack functions on all iPhone versions.

10 Hidden Shortcuts For The Favorite Apps

When you have an iPhone having a 3D Touchscreen or an iPhone 11 or more, you can find shortcuts to standard features of a few of your preferred apps hidden in the app icons. To access them, difficult to push an app symbol. When the app helps this function, a menu pops right out of the image with a couple of shortcuts. Touch the one you would like and you'll leap into the app and into that actions.

Notice: *This hack functions on the iPhone 6S collection, 7 collections, 8 collections, X, XS, XR, and 11 collections.*

11 Help to make Far-Away Icons Better to Reach

As iPhone displays get bigger, getting icons at the corner of your hands gets harder. The iOS carries a function known as Reachability that pulls the very best symbols down the underneath of the display screen to make them simpler to the faucet. Here's how:

- On iPhones with a house button, gently dual touch (but don't click on) the house button.

- On the iPhone X or more, swipe down in the indicator line at the bottom of the display.

- The contents from the screen shift down.

- Tap that you would like and the display screen dates back to normal. If you have changed your mind, tap somewhere else on the display to cancel.

This hack works on the iPhone 6 series, 6S series, 7 series, 8 series, along with the iPhone X, XS series, XR, 11, and 12 series.

12 substitute for your keyboard using a trackpad

We have a trick for you personally that makes puting the cursor in textual content easier. It functions by switching your keyboard right into a trackpad, just like the mouse on the laptop. Some tips about what to accomplish:

- Open up an app where you may edit the written text using the default iPhone keypad (quite a few third-party keyboards help this feature, as well).

- Tap and keep any key on the keyboard.

- The letters over the keys disappear. Pull your finger round the keypad like managing a mouse on the trackpad.

- View the cursor around the display screen and release once the cursor is where you need it to be.

Take note: This hack functions on iPhone versions having a 3D Touchscreen working iOS 9 or more, and on all the models operating iOS 12. On iOS 13, it is possible to just pull the cursor anyplace on the display; you don't need to hard push the keyboard.

13 Switch to Undo Typing

If you are typing an email, a text, or various other textual content and decide you intend to erase what you've simply written, you don't have to utilize the delete button on the keyboard. When you have this hack allowed, all you have to do will be switch your iPhone to delete whatsoever you have typed. Here's what to accomplish:

- Tap Settings.

- Tap Accessibility.

- Touch (in iOS 13 or more only).

- In the Interaction section, tap Shake to Undo.

- Proceed the slider to on/environment friendly.

- After that, whenever you've simply typed something you intend to remove, shake your cell phone and faucet Undo in the pop-up window.

Be aware: This hack functions on all iPhone versions.

14 Equalize Songs Quantity When One Touch

Ever observe that the songs on your cell phone are recorded at various volumes? Old tunes are often quiet, newer tunes are often louder. This may mean that you must change the quantity regularly. Well, we have a trick that makes all your songs play at the same degree. It's called Audio Check and it's included in the iOS. It inspects the quantity on all your songs finds the average and applies that to your songs automatically. Here's how to enable it:

- Tap Settings.

- Tap Music.

- Scroll right down to Playback.

- Move the Noise Examine slider to on/natural.

- This hack works on all iPhone models.

15 Measure Areas Making use of Augmented Reality

You might understand that your iPhone includes a built-in Level you should use to straighten pictures or shelves, but did you also know, it comes with an app called Gauge that uses Augmented Reality to assist you to measure distances? Some tips about what you must do:

- Tap the Gauge app to open up it.

- Place your iPhone camera so that it's dealing with a flat surface area.

- Touch the + symbol to start calculating.

- Shift the iPhone for the screen to also moves.

- When you've measured the area, touch the + once again showing the measured range.

Notice: The Gauge app can perform better than this. This hack works on the iPhone SE and 6S series and higher, running iOS 12 or more.

CHAPTER 4

Tips for Managing Your Old iPhone After an Update

Each year, Apple releases new iPhone models. You're probably upgrading your old iPhone before it reaches the end of its useful life if you always keep on the cutting edge. Prices have soared since carriers are no longer willing to subsidize iPhones as they previously did. You can get a great trade-in offer at the Apple Store and at most carriers for your old iPhone. When you update to the brand-new iPhone, there are a ton of different things you can do with your old device if you don't want to trade it in or keep it as a backup.

Transfer It

Give your old iPhone to a relative or acquaintance. Before you give the iPhone away, take out the SIM card if it is on your old phone. The recipient can take the iPhone in and the carrier will assist him in setting it up on the network, provided he choose a suitable carrier. AT&T and T-Mobile are suitable carriers if your old iPhone is a GSM phone. Both Sprint and Verizon are compatible carriers if the iPhone is a CDMA phone. How are the differences discerned? While CDMA iPhones lack SIMs, GSM iPhones do.

Make It Into a Touch iPod

Without cellular connectivity, an iPhone is basically an iPod touch. You have a media player, a contact and calendar device, and a Wi-Fi connection when you remove the SIM card, if the iPhone has one. To access the App Store and perform all of the functions of an iPod touch, the iPhone connects via Wi-Fi. Put on your favorite music and go for a jog while wearing earbuds.

The fortunate recipient of your iPod touch gift will require a free Apple ID in order for it to function. Using his Apple ID, he may download previously purchased apps and music to his new iPod touch and browse the App Store for both free and paid programs.

Transform It Into a Safety Camera

You can use your iPhone to create a security camera if it is an iPhone 5 or later. For that, you will need to download an app, but once you have it, you will have access to cloud recording, motion alerts, and live streaming. The apps are willing to offer you a storage package if you want to save and watch surveillance footage. Three apps may make your old iPhone into a security camera: the Presence app, the Manything app, and the AtHome Camera app.

Utilize It as a Remote Control for Apple TV

Should you be among those who find the included remote control unbearable, all you need to do is download the Apple TV Remote app into your outdated iPhone, and voila! You'll have a brand-new remote. If your Apple TV is newer, you can manage it with Siri on your iPhone. You can still find a lot more shows using the keyboard to search on older Apple TV versions than you can with the included remote.

Repurpose It

Any Apple product can be recycled by dropping it off at the Apple Store. You can utilize Apple GiveBack online to send in a prepaid mailing label that Apple will send you if you don't live close to an Apple Store. Apple guarantees that every component in your phone will be recycled ethically.

If only you could recycle your old iPhone and earn some cash in the process. You can wait. Apple will recycle eligible phones and give you an Apple gift card if your iPhone is an iPhone 4s or newer. You must visit Apple's recycling page and provide information about your model, including its capacity, color, and condition. Apple then estimates its value for you.

Sell It

There is a huge market for used iPhones on the internet. Simply type in "iPhone resellers" and see what results up. It is likely that you will have little issue selling the phone if you set your pricing reasonably. Old favorites like eBay and Craigslist are good options to explore when looking for locations to sell the iPhone. To get the best deal and the easiest transaction possible, make sure to utilize other people's advice and experience with such stores.

To find out how much your old iPhone is worth, use Amazon's trade-in program. Send in the phone, and without any trouble, Amazon will offer you Amazon credit for the agreed-upon sum. Smaller internet retailers might be worth your consideration because they might face less competition. In that scenario, look for online resale options that are exclusive to mobile phones or Macs.

In either case, make sure you remove all of your personal information from the iPhone before giving it to someone else.

Note: See How to Prepare Your iPhone For Sale for a comprehensive guide on selling an old iPhone or other Apple device.

How to Set Up Your iPhone to Detect Face Recognition

Activate the Find My

The first step in setting up an iPhone is the Find My option. Maybe you turned it on then. If not, turn it on by following these instructions.

- Navigate to Settings.

- Press your moniker.

- Press Find My. (To enable the feature in previous iOS versions, tap iCloud > Find My Phone.)

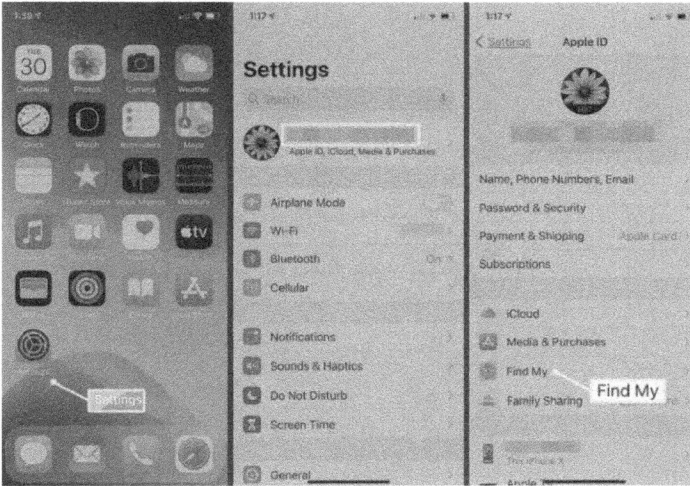

- Turn on Share My Location in the Find My screen to share your location with friends and family. To locate your phone, you do not need to enable this optional feature.

- Located at the top of the screen, tap Find My iPhone.

- Toggle the Find My iPhone switch on.

- You can view your phone even when it is offline by

turning on the Find My network setting. To locate the gadget, you do not need to use this setting.

NOTE: To assist in locating your device, the Find My Network is an encrypted, anonymous network of Apple devices.

- To enable the phone to send Apple its location when the battery is low, turn on Send Last Location. Additionally, this setting is not required.

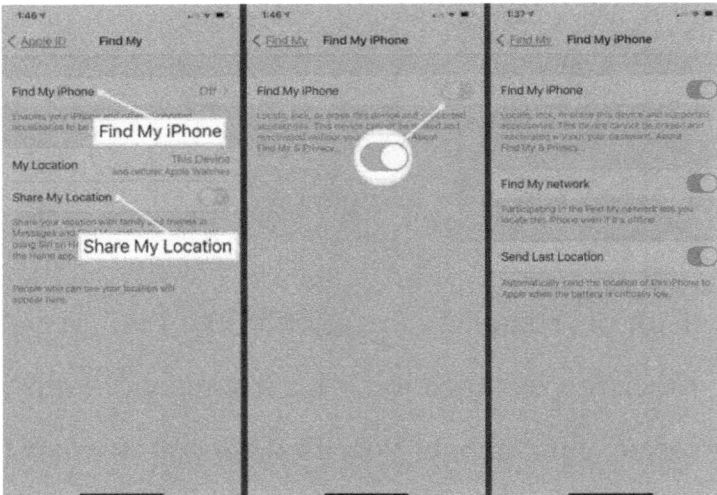

Important: To find the location of your phone on a map, you must have Location Services enabled. To verify its activation, navigate to Settings > Privacy.

NOTE: To maintain the most recent version of the material across all of your devices, set up Find My after you've done so on your phone and any other compatible devices you own.

Depending on your iOS version, you might get a notification asking you to confirm that you understand that this program tracks your iPhone's GPS. You are the one using the GPS tracking; nobody else is following you around. Click "Allow."

How to Utilize Find My

Use Find My using iCloud to find your iPhone or other iOS device if it disappears—whether it was stolen or lost.

- Launch a web browser, navigate to iCloud.com, and sign in using your iCloud account ID—also known as your Apple ID.

- Choose "Find iPhone." You might be prompted for your password once more.

- Your iPhone and any other devices you set up with Find My can be found by iCloud and shown on a map. The device is online when there is a green dot on it. If there's a gray dot, it's offline.

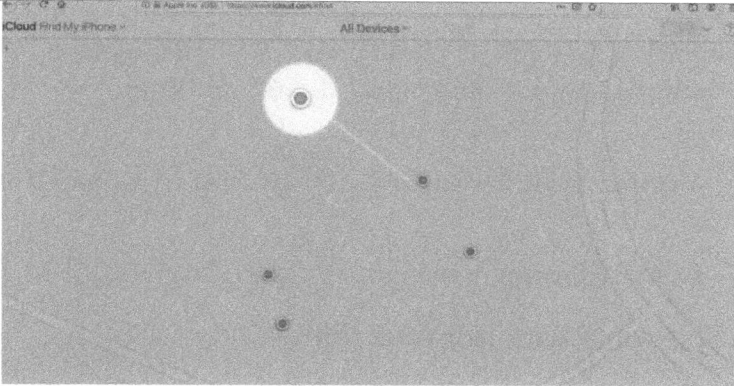

NOTE: The Apple Watch, Mac laptops, and all iOS devices are compatible with Find My. If an iOS device is nearby and AirPods are associated with it, they can be found.

- To display the missing iPhone on the map, select All Devices and then select the device.

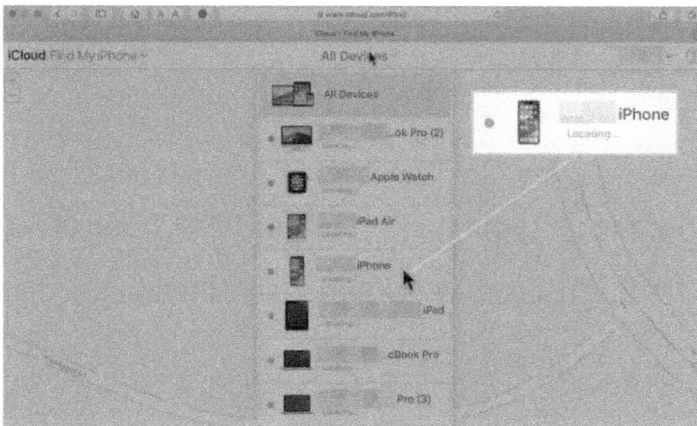

- Select one of the following options:

➢ Play Sound: Choose Play Sound and follow the sound to your suspected nearby iPhone.

➢ Your iPhone is tracked and locked in Lost Mode.

➢ Erase iPhone: You can remotely delete all of your personal data from the iPhone.

➢ Simultaneously disable Find My iPhone.

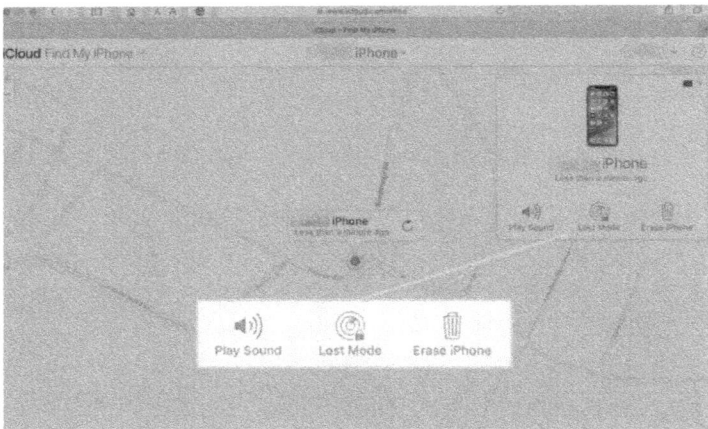

Go to Settings > [your name] > Find My > Find My iPhone, select Turn Off Find My iPhone, and then press the Back button.

In certain previous iterations of Find My iPhone, you

could be required to input the password associated with the device's iCloud account. The activation lock feature keeps thieves from disabling Find My iPhone in an attempt to conceal the handset from the service.

Find My: What Is It?

An app called Find My helps locate stolen or misplaced iPhones. It locates the device on a map by utilizing the location services or built-in GPS. To stop a burglar from accessing your data, it locks a device or erases all of its data online. Use Find My to activate the device's audio in the event that it becomes lost. To find the device, pay attention to the dinging sound.

NOTE: Apple integrated the Find My iPhone and Find My Friends functions into a single app called Find My with the release of iOS 13.

Methods for Transferring Messages Between iPhones

This tutorial shows you how to move your iMessage and SMS messages from your old iPhone to a new one. The pre-installed texting program called Messages on the iPhone is covered in the instructions. Third-party texting apps, including WhatsApp, are not covered.

How to Send and Receive Text Messages Between iPhones Using iCloud Messages

Using Messages in iCloud is possibly the easiest way to move text messages from one iPhone to another. iOS 11.4 brought this iCloud functionality. Once you enable it, all other devices logged into the same account can download messages from iCloud. This is exactly how iCloud syncing for other data operates: you upload stuff to iCloud. It's really basic and works with both iMessages and regular SMS texts. This is what you should do:

- To access Settings on your current iPhone, touch on it.

Advice: As uploading your messages will probably be quicker when connected to Wi-Fi, you might wish to be in that state. Uploading over a cellular network is acceptable in an emergency, though.

- Press your moniker.

- Press iCloud.

- Set the Messages slider to "green" or "on." The process of backing up your communications to your iCloud account is now underway.

- To transfer messages to a new phone, log into your existing iCloud account and follow the instructions to enable Messages in iCloud on the new phone. The texts from iCloud will be downloaded to the new phone automatically.

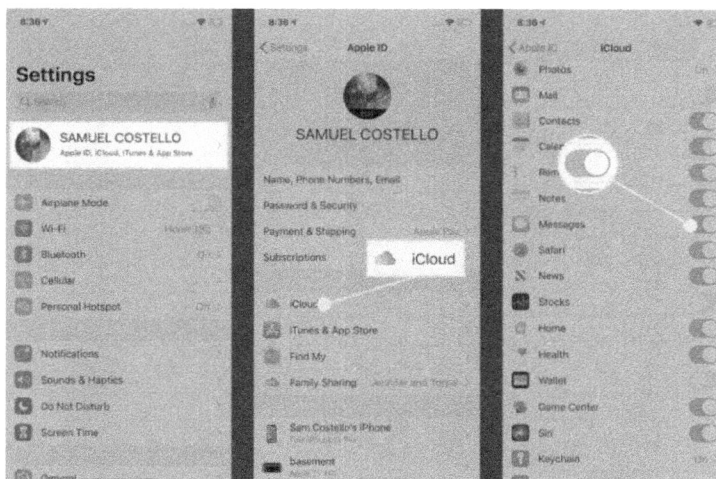

Using iCloud Backup to Receive Text Messages on Your New iPhone: A Guide

You can move messages from iPhone to iPhone by restoring from backup if you don't want to utilize Messages in iCloud for any reason—you have an older phone, you don't want your texts kept in the cloud, you don't want to pay for additional iCloud storage, etc. This is what you should do:

- Select Settings on your existing iPhone.

- Press your moniker.

- Press iCloud.

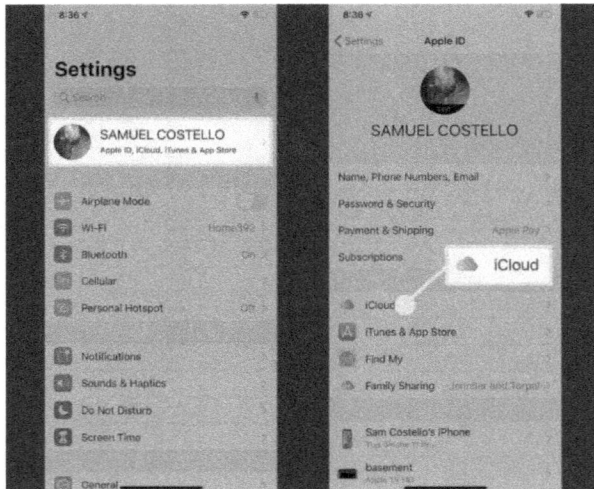

- Click on iCloud Backup.

- Slider for iCloud Backup should be on or green.

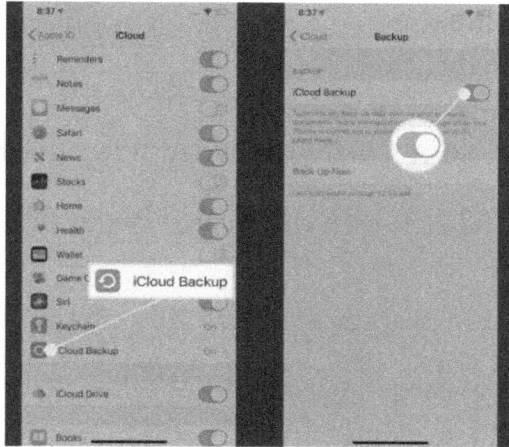

- To begin backing up immediately, tap Back Up Now. The amount of data you need to back up will determine how long this takes. Your iCloud storage may also need to be upgraded, depending on the size of the backup.

Advice: If you leave this unchecked, backups will occur automatically while your phone is charged, linked to Wi-Fi, and has its screen locked.

- Setup your new iPhone once the backup is finished. When prompted to select how to configure it, select restore from backup. Select the recently created iCloud backup, and your entire backed-up data—including messages—will be downloaded onto your new iPhone.

How to Use a Computer or Mac to Receive Text Messages on Your New iPhone

Want to move messages to a new iPhone but would rather not backup to iCloud? Utilize the tried-and-true technique of backing up your files to a PC or Mac. How to do it is as follows:

hints: Mac computers running macOS Catalina (10.15) or later should refer to the instructions. The steps are basically the same for older versions, with the exception that you back up using iTunes rather than the Finder.

- Link your Mac or PC to your existing iPhone.

- Launch a fresh instance of iTunes (for PCs) or the Finder (for Macs). Move on to step 5 if you're using a PC.

Note: As soon as your iPhone is linked to a PC running iTunes, iTunes ought to initiate an automatic backup of your device.

- If it's not already open, expand the left-hand sidebar's Locations section. Then press the iPhone button.

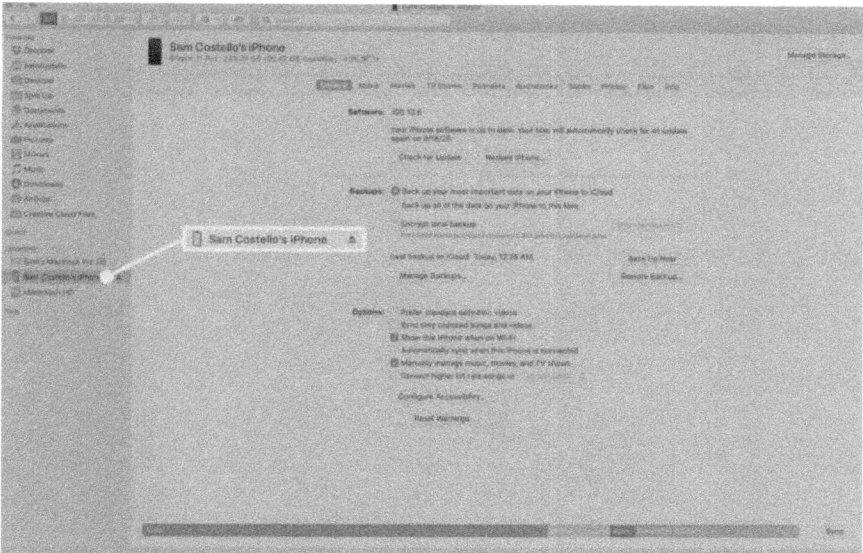

- Click Back Up Now from the iPhone management screen that displays.

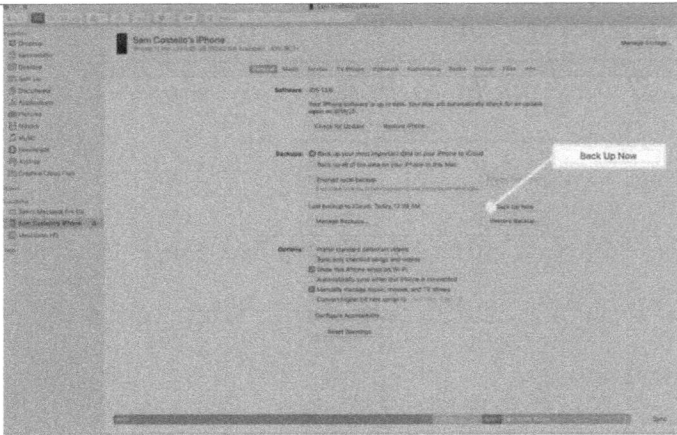

Setup your new iPhone once the backup is finished. Select Restore from backup when prompted for setup. After connecting your iPhone to the PC you just used to do the backup, choose the backup. Your texts and all other backed-up data will be downloaded to your new iPhone.

Chapter 5

26 Techniques for Increasing iPhone Battery Life

The majority of iPhones require recharging every few days, if not every day. Turning off services and features is one technique to extend the life of an iPhone battery. There are other alternatives as well. Seeing your iPhone's battery life represented as a percentage can help you keep track of it more conveniently.

1. Stop the Background App Refresh

The iPhone is more intelligent and prepared when you need it thanks to a number of features. The Background App Refresh function is one of these. This tool examines which of your apps you use most frequently and when. After that, it updates those apps so that you always have the most recent information available when you open one of them. For instance, iOS recognizes when you browse social media at 7:30 a.m. and refreshes social apps

149

immediately before then. Battery drain occurs from this helpful feature.

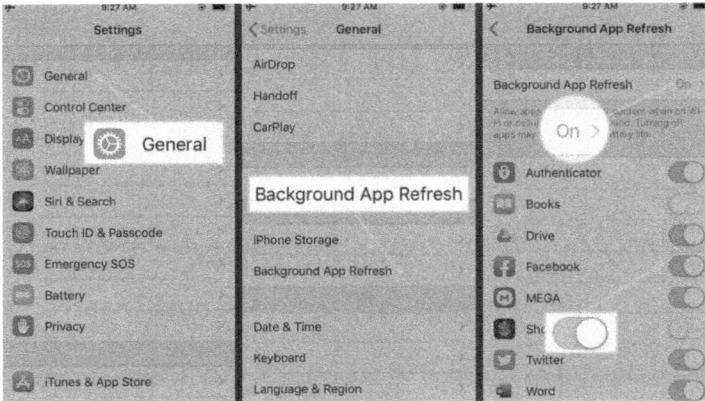

Open the Settings app, select General > Background App Refresh, and then select Background App Refresh > Off to disable Background App Refresh on the iPhone. Alternately, turn the feature off for just certain programs.

2. Invest on an Extended Life Battery.

Purchasing more battery for your iPhone is another method to prolong its life. Manufacturers of accessories like Mophie provide iPhone batteries with an enhanced lifespan. An extended life battery gives extra days of standby time and more hours of use if you require so much battery life that none of these suggestions work for you.

3. Avoid Using Automatic App Updates

Turn off the feature that updates apps automatically when new versions are published if you're using iOS 7 or later. This is both a battery drainer and a convenience. When the battery is completely charged, update apps manually; otherwise, disable automated app updates.

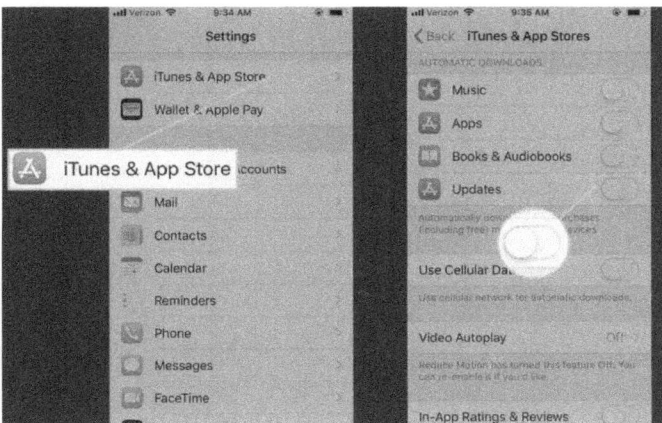

Go to Settings > App Store and disable App Updates to disable automatic app updates. This setting may be found in the iTunes & Apps settings in previous iterations of iOS.

4. Never Accept App Suggestions

With iOS 8, Suggested Apps uses your location to determine your current position and the objects nearby. Based on your current location, it utilizes this data to suggest apps to you. Receive alerts from Walgreens, for instance, when one of those stores is nearby.

In order to keep track of your position and interact with the App Store, this feature takes more battery life. It might not be on, but if it is, you should turn it off.

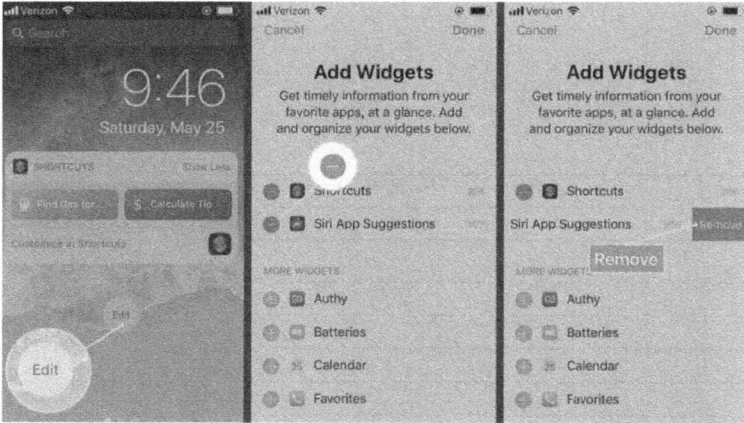

Swipe left to get the Today view from the Home screen, then scroll to the bottom of the screen and choose Edit to turn off Suggested Apps. To remove Siri App Suggestions, tap the red icon next to it and select Remove.

5. Utilize Safari's content blockers

Blocking tracking cookies and advertisements in Safari is one of the coolest new features in iOS 9. A lot of battery life is used by the technologies that advertising networks use to supply, show, and track ads.

Blocking cookies and advertisements doesn't save as much battery life as other battery-saving advice. However, the Safari browser uses less bandwidth and operates faster, in addition to a little increase in battery life.

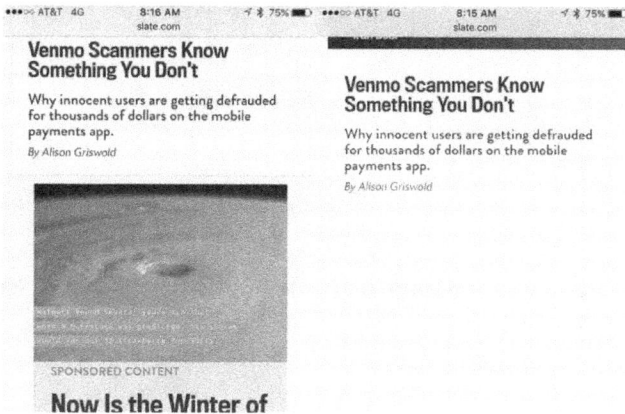

To utilize these privacy and security measures that save battery life, go to Settings > Safari and toggle on Prevent Cross-Site Tracking, Block All Cookies, and Privacy Preserving Ad Measurement.

6. Activate Auto-Brightness.

The iPhone's ambient light sensor modifies the screen's brightness according to the surrounding light. This sensor adjusts the screen's brightness to make it brighter in brighter environments and darker in darker ones. This feature makes the phone easier to operate while conserving battery life.

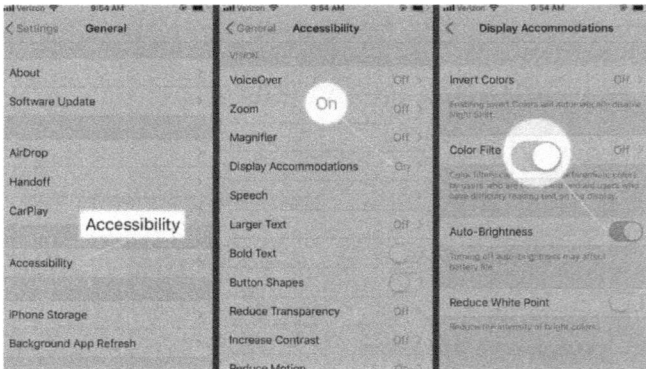

To save energy, activate Auto-Brightness so that your screen will use less power in less lit areas.

In iOS 13 and later, open the Settings app, select Accessibility > Display & Text Size, scroll down, then tap Auto-Brightness to enable Auto-Brightness.

Navigate to Settings > General > Accessibility > Display Accommodations in iOS 12 and iOS 11, then select Auto-Brightness.

To enable Auto-Brightness on iOS 10 and below, launch the Settings app, select Display & Brightness (or Brightness & Wallpaper in iOS 7), and then confirm the setting.

7. Animations & Stop Motion

The Background Motion feature in iOS 7 is one of the best additions. It's subtle: As you move the iPhone, you'll notice that the background image and app icons move separately, as though they are on separate planes.

The phone appears more alive thanks to this parallax effect, which is fun to demonstrate. Nevertheless, it depletes an iPhone's battery and delivers minimal functionality. In addition, some people's motion sickness may be lessened by turning off this additional motion on an iPhone.

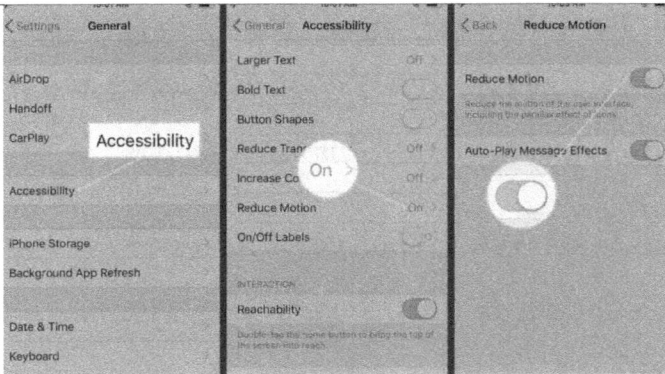

In iOS 12 and later, enter Settings, select Accessibility > Motion, and toggle on Reduce Motion to disable Background Motion.

To enable Reduce Motion on iOS 11 and below, navigate to Settings > General > Accessibility > Reduce Motion, and then click on it.

8. Turn off WiFi while it's not in use.

If the Wi-Fi signal is stronger than the cellular signal, Wi-Fi offers advantages and can prolong battery life. It can deplete the battery to always have Wi-Fi enabled in order to locate an open hotspot. Whenever Wi-Fi is accessible, connect to it. Turn down Wi-Fi on your iPhone to conserve battery life if you're not near a Wi-Fi network, such as when traveling.

Go to Settings > Wi-Fi and flip the switch to turn off Wi-Fi. As an alternative, you can swipe up from the bottom or down from the top of the screen, depending on the type of your iPhone, and then hit the Wi-Fi icon to turn it gray.

Note: The Apple Watch is not covered by this advice. Don't turn off Wi-Fi; it's necessary for many Apple Watch functionalities.

9. Verify That Your Personal Hotspot Is Off.

An iPhone may be made into a hotspot by using Personal Hotspot, which allows it to broadcast its cellular data to other nearby devices. Although it is a helpful function, the battery is also depleted by it. particularly if, after using the hotspot for a while, you forget to switch it off.

Note: There is a list of battery-saving suggestions

available when using your phone as a hotspot.

On an iPhone, to disable the hotspot, open the Settings app, select Personal Hotspot, and then flip off the toggle switch for Personal Hotspot.

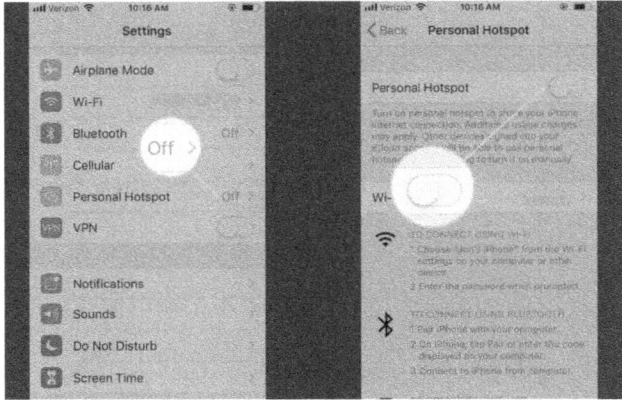

10. Track Down the Battery Killers

The Battery Usage feature in iOS 8 and later releases displays the apps that have consumed the most power over the past several days and the past 24 hours. To check, navigate to Settings > Battery. Underneath each item, there can be notes explaining why the program used so much battery life and offering solutions.

Remark: If an application is frequently used, it consumes a lot of battery life if it is regularly listed.

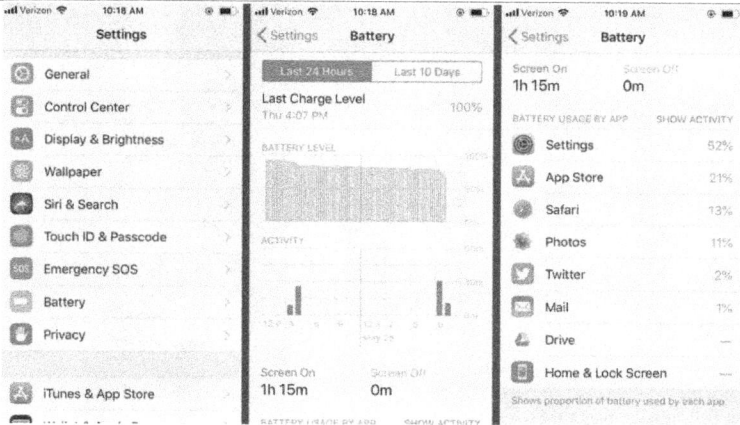

11. Disable Location Services

The GPS incorporated into the iPhone locates surrounding restaurants, shops, and other locations and provides directions. It requires battery power to operate, though, just like any other service that transmits data over a network. Turn off Location Services if you're not using it to conserve electricity.

Open the Settings app, navigate to Privacy > Location Services, choose Location Services, and then press Turn Off to totally deactivate Location Services. Alternatively, go down the page and block certain apps' Location Services.

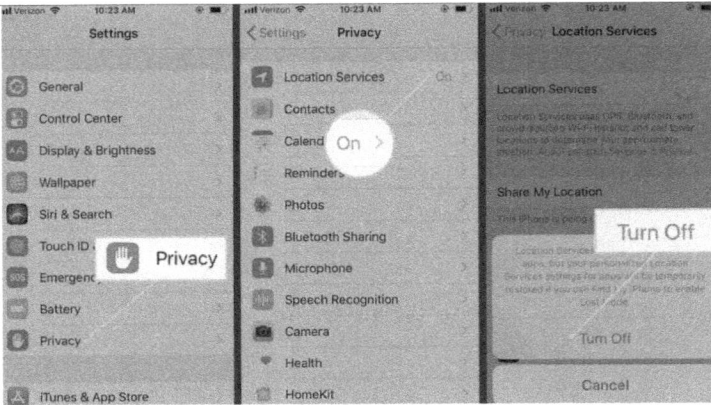

12. Disable Additional Location Configurations

Numerous actions are completed by the iPhone in the background. The battery is quickly depleted by background activity, particularly when it involves using GPS or an internet connection. To extend the life of the battery, features that aren't needed can be safely disabled.

Navigate to Settings > Privacy > Location Services > System Services, disable Location-Based Apple Ads, Popular Near Me, and Set Time Zone to stop background tasks.

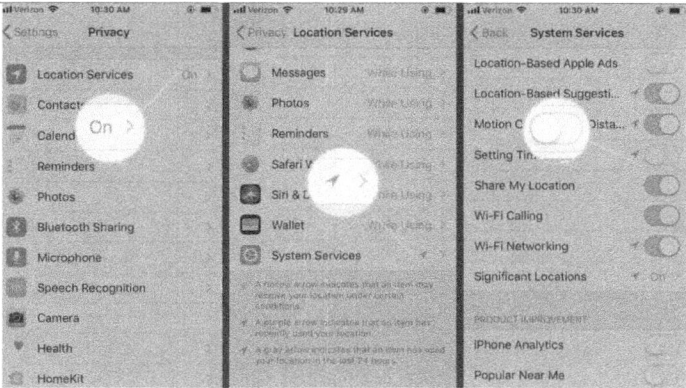

When you disable all location services, these choices are not accessible.

13. Avoid Using Changing Backgrounds

With iOS 8, live and dynamic wallpapers were introduced, providing a clean interface in contrast to a static background image. Battery life is also impacted by these wallpapers. Restricting your iPhone's background to still images is a simple technique to extend its battery life.

Since there is no way to enable or disable dynamic backgrounds, they do not need to be turned off. Instead, while you're updating the iPhone wallpaper, avoid selecting any photographs from the Dynamic section.

14. Switch off Bluetooth.

Bluetooth works well with wireless headphones and earbuds, but it uses a lot of battery power to transfer data wirelessly and more power to keep Bluetooth enabled all the time to receive incoming data. To save your iPhone's battery, turn off Bluetooth. Alternatively, turn off Bluetooth while not in use and only activate it when necessary.

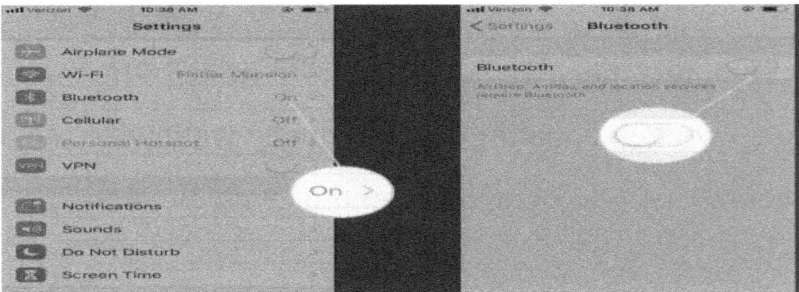

On an iPhone, the Settings app's Bluetooth section contains the ability to enable or disable Bluetooth.

Note: The Apple Watch is not compatible with our iPhone battery-saving advice. Through Bluetooth, the iPhone and Apple Watch can connect. Make sure Bluetooth is on your wristwatch to get the most out of it.

15. Disable Cellular Data

The phone's battery has to be used more when using 5G, 4G, LTE, or any other cellular connection with fast transfer speeds. During periods of high usage, such as while making HD calls or streaming videos, the power consumption increases. Even though it can be difficult, stopping all cellular data transfers will extend the iPhone's battery life.

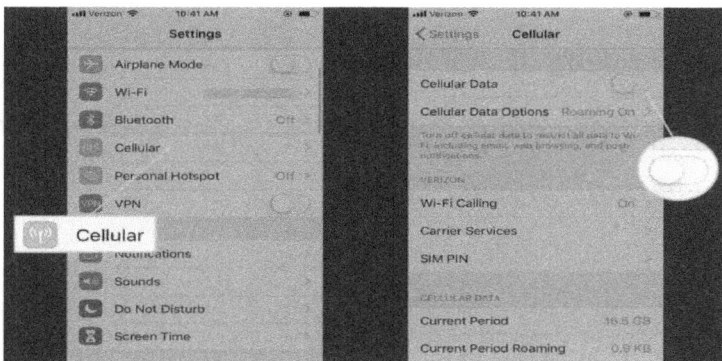

Open Settings, select Cellular, and then select Cellular Data to disable cellular data.

Advice: Even if cellular data is disabled, Wi-Fi continues to function.

16. Activate Data Push Off

An iPhone's email settings can be set up to download messages to the device automatically as soon as they are received from the email server. While having up-to-date email folders is helpful, the battery is depleted more quickly by continuous downloads. To check for new messages, open the Mail app and manually refresh it.

Open the Settings app, pick Fetch New Data, tap Passwords & Accounts (or Mail > Accounts), then switch off Push to save the iPhone's battery life.

Note: Changing the frequency at which your iPhone checks for fresh mail is another way to conserve battery life on an email-enabled iPhone.

Settings | < Passwords & Accounts | < Back Fetch New Data

iTunes & App Store

Wallet & Apple Pay

Passwords & Accounts

Mail

Passwords & Accounts

Calendar

Reminders

Phone

Messages

FaceTime

iCloud Drive, Contacts and 10 more

Exchange
Inactive

Outlook
Inactive

Yahoo!
Mail

Zoho
Inactive

Work
Mail

Gmail
Inactive

Add Account

Fetch New Data   Automatically

Fetch New Data

Push

New data will be pushed to your iPhone from the server when possible

Yahoo!
Mail

Work
Mail

iCloud
iCloud Drive, Contacts and 10 more

Holiday Calendar
Calendars

Jon Fisher
Contacts, Calendars

FETCH

The schedule below is used when push is off or

Fetch >

Fetch >

Fetch >

Fetch >

Fetch >

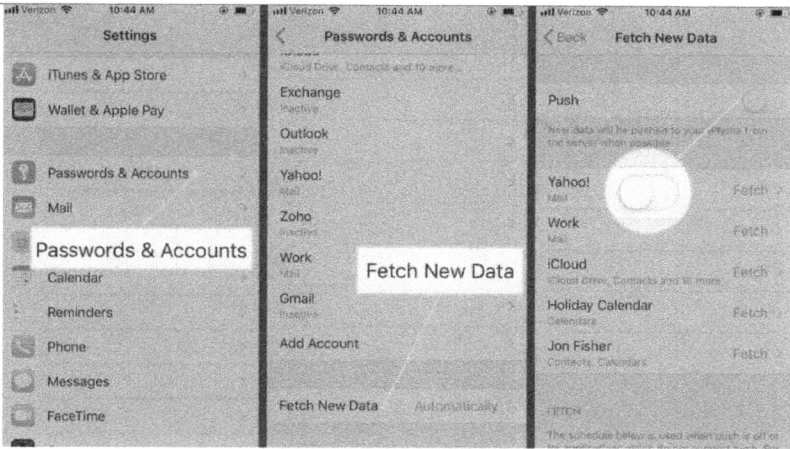

17. Auto-Lock Early

Early phone auto-locking conserves battery life. A phone that continuously shows content, regardless of brightness level, needs electricity all the time. Locking the phone is a simple remedy, but you can also modify the auto-lock option to make it lock on its own.

Select the auto-lock option that best suits your needs. Battery life is increased by anything less than Never; the more often the lock is maintained, the longer the battery will last.

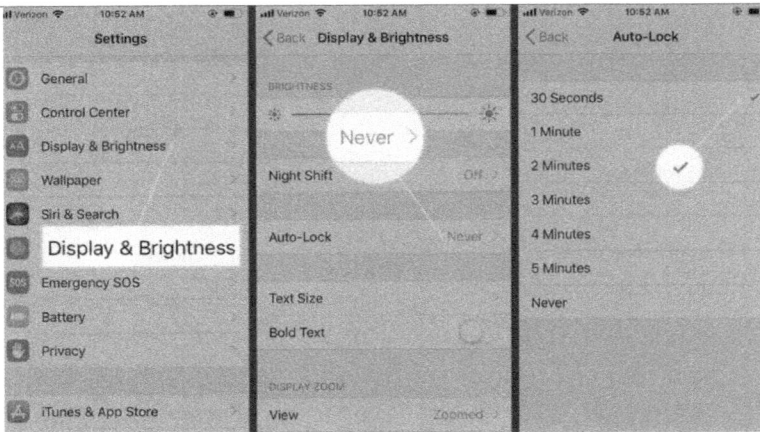

Note: Open the Settings app, hit Display & Brightness, pick Auto-Lock, and then enter a time between 30 and 5 minutes to set the auto-lock.

18. Disable the Fitness Tracking

The iPhone 5S and later versions can track steps and other fitness activities thanks to the addition of a motion co-processor. For people who wish to maintain their fitness, it's a fantastic function. However, continuous tracking necessitates battery life.

If you don't use your iPhone for motion tracking and you own a fitness band, you may stop the feature by going to Settings > Privacy (or Privacy & Security) > Motion & Fitness and turning off Fitness Tracking.

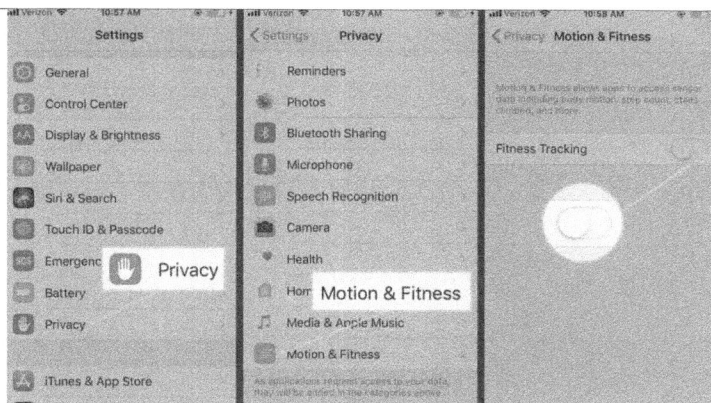

19. Switch off the equalizer.

The Equalizer tool in the iPhone Music app allows you to alter the audio by boosting the bass, lowering the treble, and making other adjustments. These changes use more battery power because they are made dynamically. To save battery life, turn off the equalization. Disabling the equalizer, however, results in a slightly different listening experience.

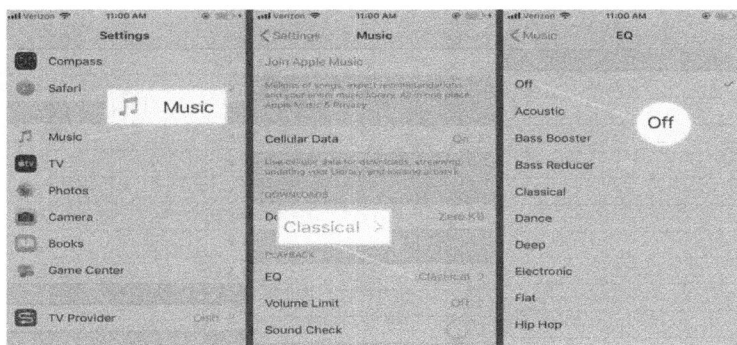

To disable the equalizer on your iPhone and preserve battery life, enter Settings and select Music > EQ > Off.

20. Turn Off Cell Phone Calls From Other Devices

You can use the cellular connection on your iPhone to place and receive calls through your Mac if both devices are connected to the same Wi-Fi network. Using this option makes the Mac function as an iPhone extension, but it also depletes the iPhone's battery.

Note: Only Macs running OS X 10.10 (Yosemite) or later and iPhones running iOS 8 or later are compatible with this advice.

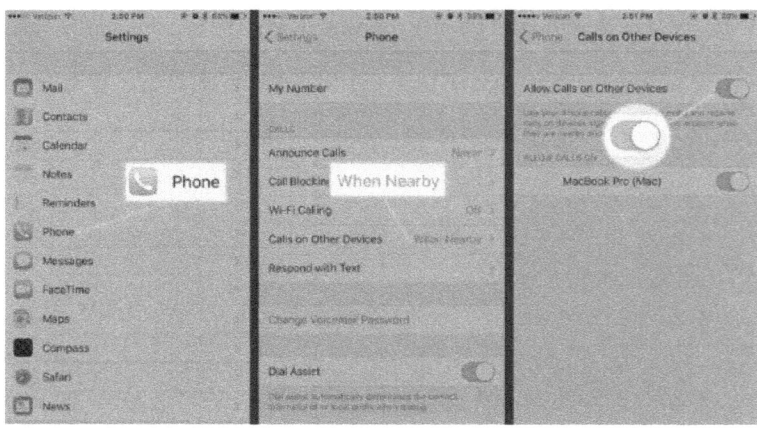

Navigate to Settings > Phone > Calls on Other Devices,

choose Allow Calls on Other Devices, and then click "OK" to disable this option.

21. Turn off AirDrop when not in use.

Apple introduced AirDrop, a wireless file-sharing capability in iOS 7, and it can be very useful. Turn on Wi-Fi and Bluetooth on an iPhone, then configure the device to search for other devices that support AirDrop. Any feature that employs wireless technologies will use more battery life the more you use it. When not in use, turn off AirDrop on your iPhone to conserve battery life.

Using the Control Center, you can turn on and off AirDrop reception. After swiping up or down from the top or bottom of the screen, select AirDrop. Select Receiving Off to turn it off.

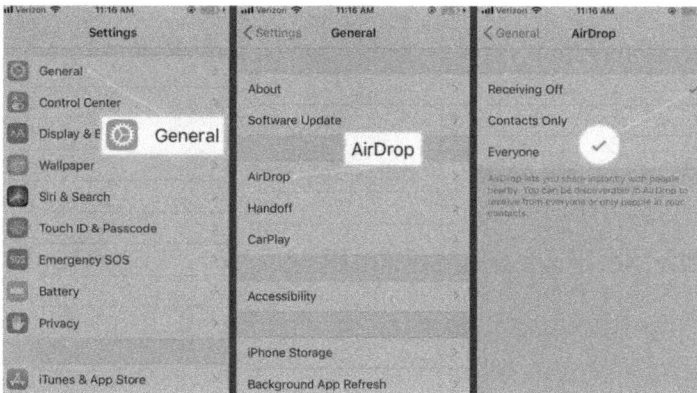

You can also adjust AirDrop's functionality by going to Settings > General > AirDrop.

22. Avoid Having Photos Uploaded to iCloud Automatically

Every time data is uploaded, the battery drains. Verify that you are uploading on purpose as opposed to having it happen on autopilot. This is the first place to look, as the Photos app has the ability to upload photos to your iCloud account automatically. Only upload from your PC or when your battery is fully charged; turn off auto-uploads.

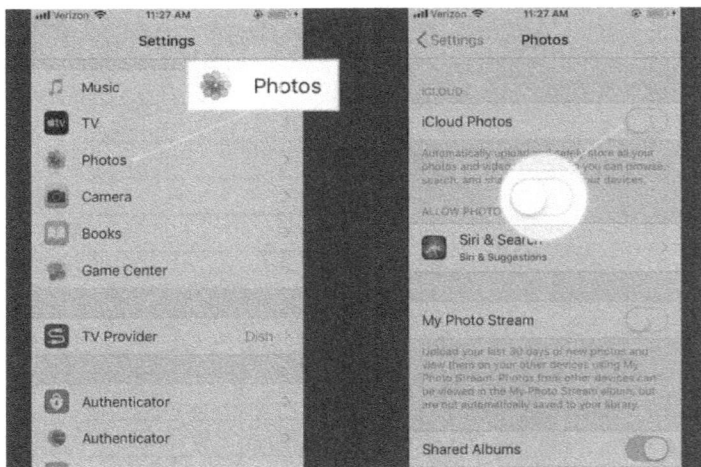

Open the Settings app, select Photos (or Photos & Camera on earlier devices), and then disable iCloud Photos or iCloud Photo Library to see if your photos always upload to iCloud.

23. Turn Off Superfluous Vibrations

An iPhone may vibrate to draw your attention to calls and other notifications, but in order for the phone to do so, the battery must be used to start a motor that rattles the device. The vibration is not required if the device has a specified ringtone or alert tone.

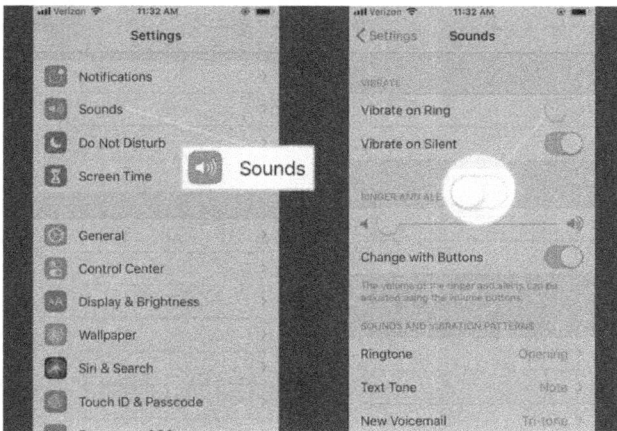

Use vibration just when required, such as when the ringer is off, as opposed to leaving it on constantly. Open Settings, select Sounds (or Sounds & Haptics), and then disable Vibrate on Ring to disable this feature.

24. Employ Low Power Mode

Try Low Power Mode, a feature added in iOS 9, if you need to save battery life on your iPhone but don't want to disable settings one at a time.

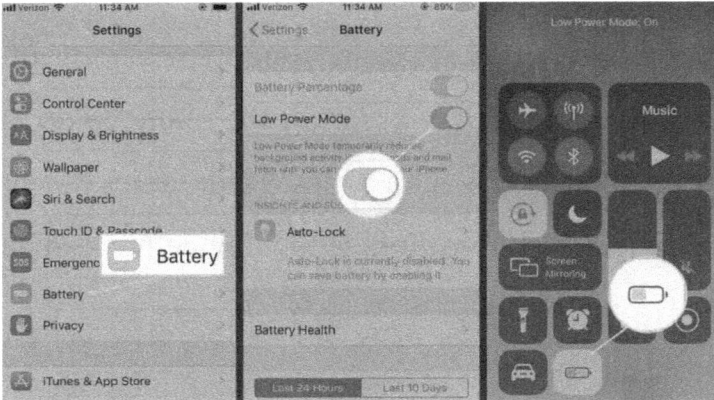

In order to save as much battery as possible, the iPhone's Low battery Mode turns off all non-essential functionalities. According to Apple, activating this will extend battery life by up to three hours.

Go to Settings > Battery and enable Low Power Mode. You can also use Control Center; to enable or disable it, just hit the battery icon.

25. Reduce How Often You Close Apps

It is not advantageous to leave apps open in the background when you are finished with them. Shutting off apps on a regular basis might accelerate battery consumption. Frequently relaunching an application consumes more battery life than allowing it to operate in the background.

When you're not using an app, leave it open to conserve battery life.

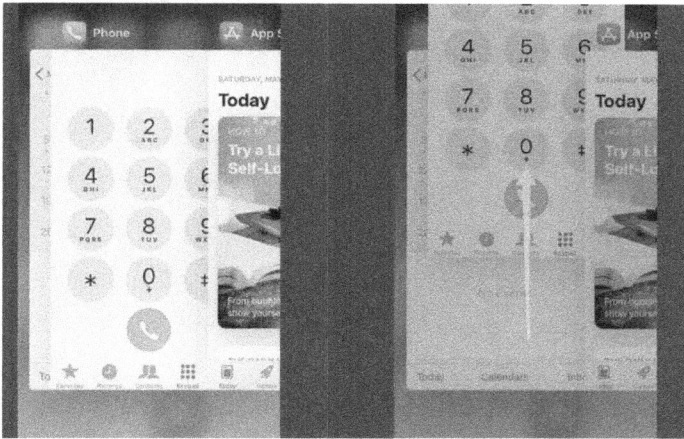

26. Deplete your battery as much as you can

The iPhone battery loses capacity the more often it is charged. The battery eventually learns to recognize the point of drain at which you replenish it and begins to regard that as its maximum capacity. When charging an iPhone at 75% of its remaining battery life, for instance, the battery will begin to act as though it had 75% of its original capacity left, rather than 100%.

This kind of battery drain can be avoided by using the phone for as long as possible before charging it. Prior to charging, wait till the phone's battery is 20% (or less) low.

Be aware that not all iPhones can charge wirelessly. Wireless phone charging does not extend battery life, and if you choose a slow charger, it may take longer to fully charge an iPhone.

Nine Pointers to Examine Before Buying a Used iPhone

Although the iPhone is a fantastic gadget, they are pricey

and infrequently go on sale. Therefore, purchasing a used iPhone can be your best option if you want to purchase an iPhone without having to spend full price. Although a used iPhone can be a great value, there are nine factors you should consider before making a purchase, as well as some advice on where to look for a decent offer.

Are Refurbished iPhones Reputable and Good?

Buying an iPhone that has been reconditioned or used may raise some worries for you. It makes sense to question if a used iPhone is just as dependable and high-quality as a brand-new one. That relies on where you get the iPhone, is the response. You can presume that an iPhone that has been refurbished is an excellent iPhone if you're purchasing from a seasoned, reliable, and established supplier (think Apple and phone firms). Increase your suspicions about less reliable sellers.

Choose the Appropriate Phone for Your Phone Company

The iPhone 5 and subsequent variants are compatible with all phone carrier networks. That being said, it's helpful to know that AT&T's network makes use of an additional LTE signal than the others, which in some locations may result in speedier service. Purchase an iPhone made for Verizon, and then bring it to AT&T, and you might not be able to use that additional LTE signal. Make that the iPhone is compatible with your phone carrier by asking the vendor for the model number, which should be something like A1633 or A1688).

Verify That the Pre-owned iPhone Isn't Stolen

You don't want to purchase a stolen phone while purchasing a used iPhone. With its Activation Lock function, which is enabled when Find My iPhone is activated, Apple stops new users from activating stolen iPhones. You won't be able to unlock an iCloud-locked iPhone until after you purchase the phone, which is when you'll find out if it's activation locked.

Nevertheless, you can check to see whether an iPhone is stolen before making a purchase. Depending on the provider, you will want the phone's IMEI or MEID number. To obtain it, ask the merchant for it or take the following actions:

- On the iPhone, tap the Settings app.

- Press General.

- Press & Hold.

- To find the number, scroll down and check next to IMEI (or MEID). Typically, it is a 15-digit number.

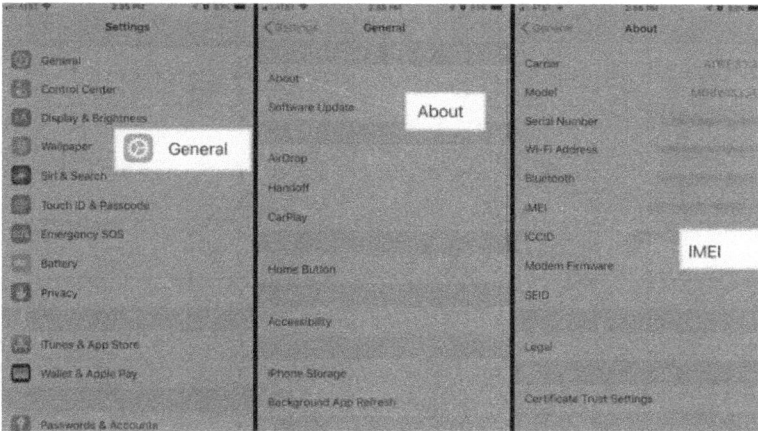

- Once you have the number, put it in the designated field on the CTIA Stolen Phone Checker website.

- After selecting "I'm not a robot" by checking the box, press Submit.

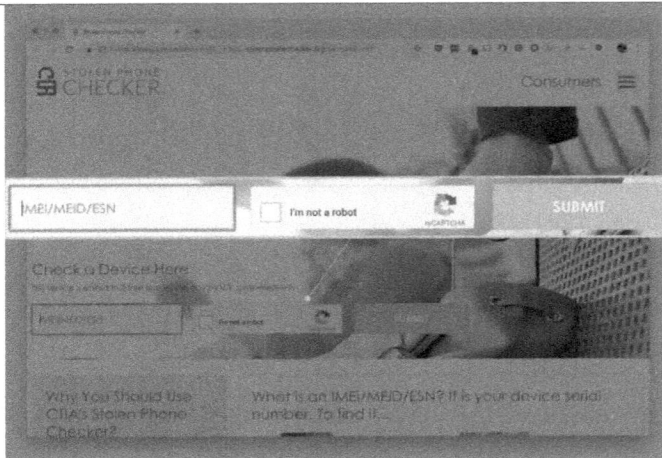

- The phone may show up on the website as not reported lost or stolen in green or as reported lost or stolen in red.

It's best to hunt for a new iPhone elsewhere if the report includes anything but the green notification.

Advice: If you're having difficulties activating a used iPhone, consider these standard troubleshooting techniques, such disabling Activation Lock.

Verify the phone isn't locked to a carrier.

Before making a purchase, even if you have the correct iPhone model, it's a good idea to check with your phone provider that it can activate the device. Use the methods above to find the phone's IMEI or MEID number, or ask the seller how to do it. Next, give your carrier a call, explain the circumstances, and provide the IMEI or MEID number of the phone. If the phone is compatible, the company ought to be able to tell you.

Verify the battery of the used iPhone.

Make sure the secondhand iPhone you purchase has a robust battery because it isn't practical to replace the iPhone's battery. A lightly used iPhone should have a respectable amount of battery life, but if it's older than a year, you should check.

Here's how to make use of iOS 12 and later phones' Battery Health feature.

- Press the Settings application.

- Press the battery.

- Select Battery Health.

- You can determine the quality of the battery by looking at the percentage shown in the Maximum Capacity section. The closer you are to 100%

capacity—the ideal state for a brand-new phone's battery—the better.

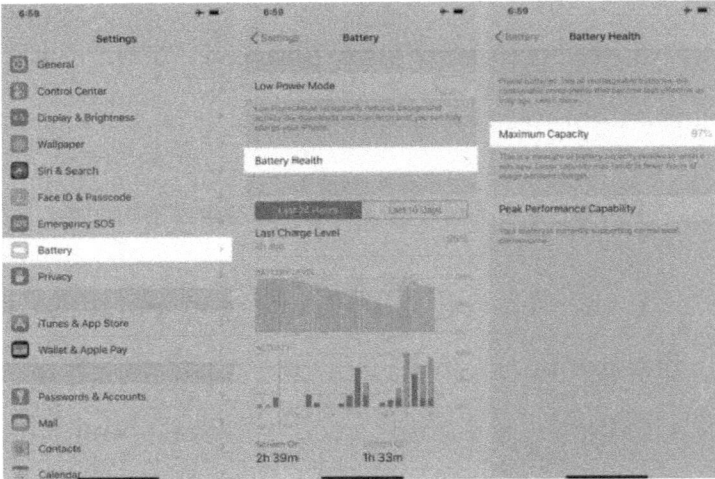

If you can't find a trustworthy source for information on the condition, you can replace the battery in your iPhone at a fair price by visiting Apple.com to acquire a price quote before making a purchase.

Examine any more hardware damage.

Every iPhone has typical wear and tear, which includes scratches and dents on the back and sides of the device. But serious screen scratches, issues with the Touch ID, Face ID, or 3D Touch sensor, scratches on the lens of the camera, or other hardware damage can be major issues. If at all feasible, request to see the phone in person.

To find out if the iPhone has ever been wet, check the moisture sensor. Check the hardware, including the camera and buttons. If you can't inspect the phone, purchase it from a reliable, well-established seller who stands behind their goods.

Select the Appropriate Storage Capacity

Although a cheap price may be quite alluring, keep in mind that secondhand iPhones are typically older models with smaller storage capacities than newer devices. Up to 512 GB of storage is available for storing your music, pictures, apps, and other data on the most recent generation of iPhones. There are several inexpensive variants with as little as 16 GB. It's a significant distinction. Although size isn't as significant as it once was, especially for those who use iCloud for music and photographs, you should always acquire at least 64 GB (the more, the better).

Evaluate the features and cost.

When purchasing a secondhand iPhone, make sure you are aware of the features you are giving up. You are probably purchasing a device that is at least one generation behind the current model (a reconditioned iPhone may cost as little as $100). That's acceptable and a wise financial move. Just make sure you are aware of the features that the model you are thinking about is missing and that you can live without them.

Compare the features of the iPhone models you are considering to make sure you are aware of everything about them, and make sure your smartphone can do the functions you need.

Obtain a Warranty If You Can

Go for a reconditioned iPhone that comes with a warranty if you can. The most trustworthy vendors guarantee their merchandise. A phone with a maintenance history won't always cause problems later on, but it might, so getting a warranty is a wise choice.

Note: To ensure that you're prepared to have your iPhone fixed if it is damaged, make sure you are aware of the terms of AppleCare and the regular iPhone warranty.

Where to Purchase a Refurbished or Used iPhone

Once you've determined that a used iPhone is the right device for you, you must choose where to pick it up. Some excellent resources for locating less expensive reconditioned iPhones are:

- *Apple:* The company's website offers reconditioned goods for sale. Although iPhones aren't always available, it's still worth checking because the options are always changing. With the same one-year warranty as new iPhones, the professionals fix Apple's refurbished models using original Apple components.

- *Phone Companies:* The majority of the big phone companies that sell new iPhones also sell reconditioned or used models that are traded in for upgrades or returned for maintenance.

- *Reselling used:* For the best deals on used iPhones, as well as protection plans, quality guarantees, and competitive prices, visit Gazelle.

- Both Craigslist and eBay are great places to get

deals online, but be cautious while shopping there. You can receive an iPhone that is faulty or doesn't have the specifications you expected from a scammer. Strive to remain with respectable, well-rated vendors.

Note: Check out more businesses that offer used iOS devices if you're interested in purchasing a used iPhone, and pick one that suits your needs. Check out our list of the top phone stores if you're looking to buy an iPhone or another brand of smartphone.

CHAPTER 6

Prioritize these 12 tasks when you receive a New iPhone.

Upon receiving a new iPhone, particularly if it's your first, you'll need to pick up a lot of new skills. However, you have to start somewhere, and the basics should be that place.

Note: Although there isn't a handbook included with the iPhone, you may get manuals for every iPhone model at Apple.com.

Upon receiving a new iPhone, this tutorial will walk you through the first 12 (or 13 if it's for a child) things you should do. Though they won't cover everything, these pointers will get you started on the path to being an iPhone expert.

Make an Apple ID.

An Apple ID, sometimes referred to as an iTunes account,

is required in order to utilize the iTunes Store or the App Store. This free account is used for many other helpful functions on the iPhone, such as iMessage, iCloud, Find My iPhone, FaceTime, Apple Music, and many other amazing technologies. It also allows you to purchase music, movies, apps, and more at iTunes. Although creating an Apple ID is technically optional, doing so will limit your ability to use many of the fantastic features of the iPhone.

Set up iTunes.

Even though iTunes is slated to be discontinued by Apple for Mac users, iTunes is much more than just a player and storage app for music. You may add and remove music, videos, images, apps, and more from your iPhone with this program.

Find out how to install iTunes on a Windows computer. If you have iTunes installed on your Mac, use it; if not, use the brand-new Music app.

Switch on the New iPhone

Activating your new iPhone should be your initial step. In just a few minutes, you may begin using the iPhone and accomplish whatever you need to. Activating the iPhone and selecting default settings for FaceTime, Find My iPhone, iMessage, and other utilities are the two main functions of the basic setup procedure.

Configure and synchronize Your iPhone

It's now time to connect your iPhone to your computer and begin adding stuff to it after setting up iTunes and your Apple ID. The article above can assist with that, whether it's with music from your music collection, ebooks, pictures, videos, or anything else. It also includes instructions on how to make folders, change the icons on your apps, and more.

Once you've synchronized via a USB cable, you can adjust your preferences and continue to sync over Wi-Fi. Alternately, use iCloud and do without wire syncing entirely.

Set up iCloud

Having iCloud makes using your iPhone much easier, especially if you have your music, apps, and other data spread over multiple computers or mobile devices. ICloud is a single tool that combines many functions, such as automatic data syncing between devices and the option to back up your data to Apple's servers and reinstall it online with just a click. You can also redownload anything you've purchased from the iTunes Store. Your purchases are therefore never really gone, even if you misplace or erase them.

For additional information regarding iCloud, see:

- FAQ for iCloud.

- Music and apps that download automatically.

- iTunes compatibility.

- How to move text messages between iPhones using iCloud.

Note: You shouldn't need to enroll in iCloud separately because setting it up is a part of the normal iPhone setup procedure.

Activate Find My iPhone

With the use of iCloud's Find My iPhone feature, you may

locate the iPhone on a map using its integrated GPS. If your iPhone ever gets stolen or lost, you'll be happy you have this. If so, you should be able to find it by locating the specific section of the roadway it is on. Giving the authorities that information is crucial if you want to attempt and retrieve a stolen phone. You must first set up Find My iPhone before you may use it in the event that your phone disappears. You will not regret it if you take that action immediately.

However, it's important to understand that having the Find My iPhone app and setting it up are two different things. It is not necessary to use the app.

Note: You shouldn't need to do this individually because setting up Find My iPhone is now a part of the normal iPhone setup procedure.

Configure Face ID or Touch ID.

The fingerprint scanner known as Touch ID is integrated into the Home button of the iPhone 5S, 6 series, 7 series, and 8 series (as well as some iPad models). The facial recognition technology included in the iPhone X and subsequent models is called Face ID. In addition to doing much more than only unlock phones, these functions also serve as a substitute for passcodes.

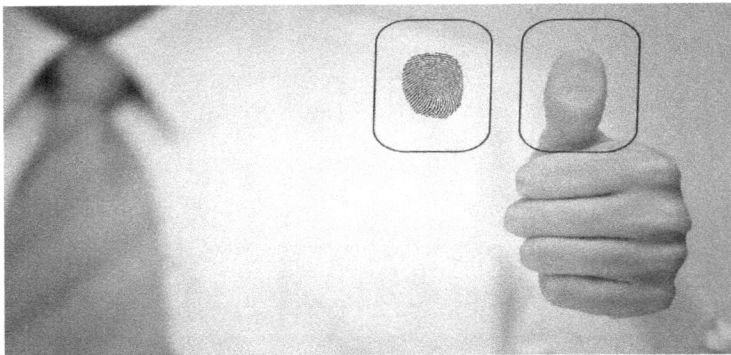

Once these are configured, you can use your finger or your face to make purchases on the iTunes or program Store. These days, any program can make use of the features. This implies that it can be used by any program that requires data security or utilizes a password. Furthermore, they serve as a crucial security component for Apple Pay, the company's wireless payment system. You should utilize whichever Touch ID or Face ID is available on your phone since they are both easy to set up and use, and they both increase the security of your phone.

Note: You shouldn't need to configure Touch ID or Face ID individually because setting them up is now a part of the normal iPhone setup procedure.

Establish Apple Pay

Apple Pay is something you should look at if you own an iPhone 6 series or later. Compared to using a regular credit or debit card, Apple's wireless payment method is far more secure, easier to use, and expedites the checkout process. There is nothing to steal because Apple Pay never gives retailers access to your actual credit card details.

Set it up and try it out if you can; not all banks provide it yet, and not all merchants take it. Once you've experienced its benefits, you'll seek for excuses to utilize it frequently.

Note: As of late, configuring Apple Pay is a part of the default iPhone setup procedure.

Create a medical ID

iPhones and other iOS devices are beginning to play significant roles in our health with the launch of the Health app in iOS 8 and later. Setting up a Medical ID is among the simplest—and possibly most beneficial—ways to take advantage of this.

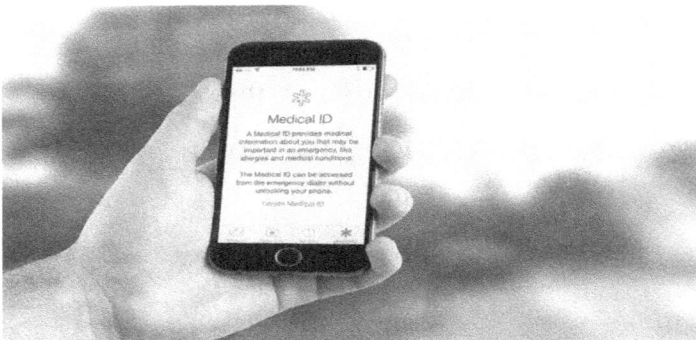

With this tool, you can include details that, in the event of a medical emergency, you would want first responders to know. This could include any information someone would need to know in order to provide you with medical care if you are unable to speak, such as the prescriptions you use, severe allergies, and emergency contacts. A medical identification card can be quite helpful, but it must be put up in advance of your need for it to be of any use.

Discover the Integrated Apps

Although the most attention is focused on the apps available in the App Store, there is also a good collection of pre-installed apps on the iPhone. Learn how to utilize the built-in apps for online surfing, email, photographs, the camera, music, calling, notes, and related utilities before delving too deeply into the App Store.

Download Fresh Apps via the App Store

After a brief exploration of the pre-installed apps, you may download a plethora of new applications from the App Store. The App Store has everything you could possibly need, including games, an app to stream Netflix on your iPhone, dinner recipe ideas, and fitness tracking software. Better yet, the majority of apps only cost one or two dollars, or perhaps nothing at all.

Check out our selections of the top apps across more than 40 categories for some ideas on what apps you might like.

When You're Prepared to Dive Further

You should now have a firm grasp on the fundamentals of using the iPhone. But the iPhone is so much more than just the essentials. It contains a wealth of entertaining and practical secrets, like how to use Control Center and Notification Center, turn on the Do Not Disturb feature, use AirPrint, and use your iPhone as a personal hotspot.

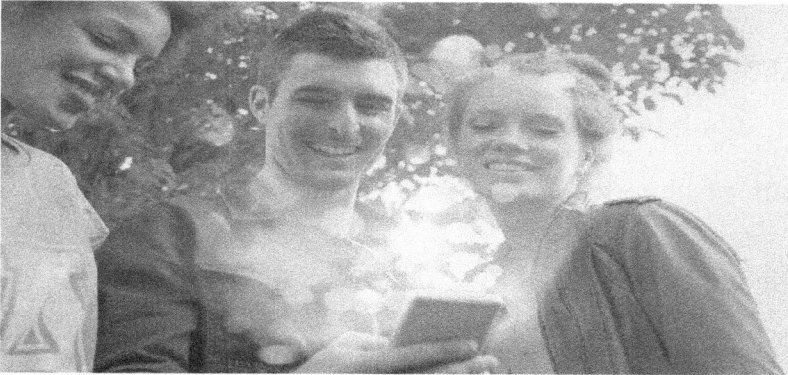

If the iPhone is meant for a child, then...

Finally, go over some crucial information to know if you're a parent and your child has the new iPhone rather than you. The iPhone is great for families because it provides parents with the means to shield their kids from potentially harmful content online, shield them from expensive iTunes Store purchases, and shield them from adult content. If you want to safeguard or insurance your child's iPhone in case it becomes misplaced or broken, you might also be interested in these options.

How to Repair and Dry a Wet iPod or iPhone

iPhones occasionally get wet. It's an inevitable part of life, regardless of our level of caution. iPhones and iPods get wet, whether we drop them in the bathtub, spill liquids on them, or have little ones who soak them in the sink.

However, a damp iPhone does not always mean that it is dead. Even if there are certain iPhones that are unsalvageable, give these suggestions a shot before writing off your cherished device.

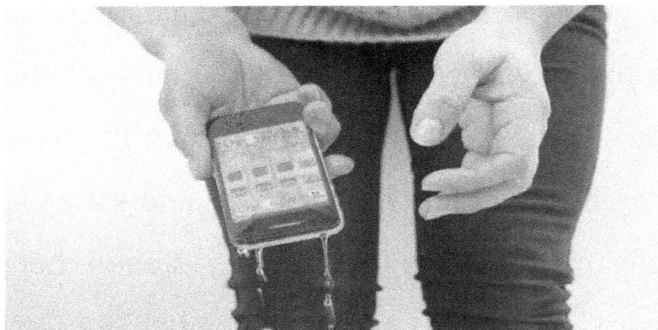

NOTE: This article's many recommendations also apply to wet iPods. We also offer all the information you need to save a damp iPad.

How to Fix a Wet iPhone and Dry It Out

To attempt to rescue your soaked iPhone, use these steps:

- Take out the case. Remove the case if your iPhone is protected by one. When there are no concealed water droplets in the case, the phone will dry more quickly and thoroughly.

- Give the water a shake. You might be able to see water in the Lightning port or headphone socket of your iPhone, depending on how wet it gets. Try to shake off as much water as you can.

- Clear it out. After shaking off the water, clean the iPhone with a soft towel to get rid of any water that may be visible. While paper towels come in handy, it's preferable to use a cloth that doesn't leave any residue behind.

- Take out the SIM card. It is best if more drying air can enter the wet iPhone. The SIM card can be removed, however the battery cannot be taken out and there aren't many other holes. Although the SIM slot is small, every little bit helps. But watch out for your SIM card!

- Put it somewhere warm. After removing as much water as you can from the phone, turn it off and place it in a warm place to dry. Certain individuals place damp iPods or iPhones on top of televisions, allowing the heat from the screen to help dry the item. Some people like their windowsills sunny. Select any strategy you desire. Give it a day or two to dry.

iPhones that are waterproof: models 7 and later

Purchasing an iPhone that is resistant to water damage in the first place is perhaps the simplest—though not the least expensive—way to save a wet one.

Water resistance is a feature shared by the iPhone X, iPhone 8 series, and iPhone 7 series smartphones. With an IP67 classification, they are resistant to damage and can withstand immersion in water up to 3.3 feet (1 meter) for up to 30 minutes.

Better further, IP68 waterproofing is available for the

iPhone XS, XR, 11 and 12 series. This indicates that they won't be harmed if submerged for 30 minutes in water up to 2, 4, and 6 meters deep, respectively.

Never Handle a Wet iPhone Like This!

What you don't do is equally as crucial as what you do if your iPhone gets wet. You might inadvertently do something that further damages your device if you're not careful. So, avoid doing the following if your iPod or iPhone is wet:

- Don't ever turn it on. You should never try to wake up or switch on an iPhone that has been water damaged. Though you might be tempted to short out its circuits and further harm them, you shouldn't do that to see if it still functions. Actually, you should stay away from anything that could interfere with the operation of the electronics, such as screen-illuminating notifications. You're good if your phone was turned off when it got wet. Turn off your device if it was on. It's a little hazardous, but better than leaving it on and using every function.

- Make no use of a hair dryer. Although some people have found success with this method, there is a chance that you could harm your gadget or disperse the water more. For the same reason, it's advisable to stay away from fans. Additionally, avoid leaving your smartphone near a radiator. That will become far too hot and may cause more damage to the phone.

More Complex Methods for Repairing a Wet iPhone

To salvage a wet iPhone, the easiest and most secure approach is to allow it to air dry. However, you can attempt the following two advanced methods to expedite the process:

- Packets of silica gel. Do you recall the small pamphlets that accompany some foods and other products and advise against eating them? They take in moisture. They help suck out moisture, if you can find enough of them to cover your damp iPhone. It could be difficult to find enough, but hardware, art supply, and craft stores are excellent options.

- Add it to the rice. The most well-known method

(albeit not always the best) is this one. Acquire some rice and a ziplock bag large enough to accommodate the damp iPhone or iPod. Reinstall the SIM card, place the gadget inside the bag, and then stuff the bag to the brim with raw rice. Put it in the bag and let it sit for a few days. The rice need to extract the moisture from the apparatus. This method has rescued many a wet iPhone. Just be cautious to prevent rice fragments from entering the phone.

Note: Steer clear of enhanced rice. Dust that is left behind may find its way inside your phone.

If you're desperate to fix your wet iPhone, don't try this.

You could try this method if you're extremely desperate or really skilled, but you really need to be careful. Both the warranty and your iPhone may be ruined.

- Disassemble it. In order to dry out the moist areas, you can disassemble your iPhone. Reassemble the device after separating the parts and letting them air dry or placing them in a bag of rice for a few days.

Note: This carries a great deal of risk. You should stay away from this unless you really, really know what you're doing, as you're likely to cause more harm than good. Say not that we warned you.

Try These Professionals for Wet iPhone Repair.

Not interested in doing this work yourself? Try the people who have repaired wet iPods and iPhones before.

- *Consider contacting a repair business.* There are iPhone repair businesses that specialize in restoring water-damaged iPhones if none of these strategies work. Spending some time on your preferred search engine can connect you with several reliable merchants.

- *Check out Apple.* Although Apple's warranty does not cover moisture damage, Apple will fix water-damaged iPhones. The cost of repairs varies depending on the model, so check this page on Apple's website for the most recent information.

How to Examine a Used iPhone or iPod for Water

Damage

Check to see if your gadget was wet if you're buying a used iPhone or iPod, or if you lent it to someone and it's not operating properly today. The iPods and iPhones' built-in moisture indicator can be used for this.

A tiny orange dot that can be found in the SIM card slot, dock connector, or headphone socket is the moisture indication. To determine the placement of the moisture indicator on your model, refer to this Apple article.

The moisture indicator is not perfect. However, if you notice the orange dot, you should at least take the possibility that the gadget didn't get along with water well.

Software Advice for Handling Wet iPhones

Your iPhone or iPod might function flawlessly and start up as if nothing had happened after you've dried it off. However, many users run into certain software issues when they initially use it. Try these suggestions for resolving some of the typical issues, which also apply to the iPad and iPod touch:

- How to Solve the Problem of an Unresponsive iPhone

- How to Unstick an iPhone from Staying at the Apple Logo.

Acknowledgments

The Glory of this book success goes to God Almighty and my beautiful Family, Fans, Readers & well-wishers, Customers and Friends for their endless support and encouragements.

Author Profile

Meet Chris Amber, the energetic writer behind "EnergyCyclist Publishing" who specializes in technology and gadget books. His love of dissecting the intricacies of modern technology has made him a respected authority in the area.

Background: Chris was eager to learn about the complex world of technology when he first started his adventure into it. Equipped with a technical studies degree, he immersed himself in the rapidly changing field of innovation, aiming to provide both enthusiasts and inquisitive minds with an understanding of the newest devices and technological breakthroughs.

Expertise: Chris has a deep understanding of the rapidly changing technology sector and focuses on producing incisive and easily understood material that helps users understand complicated technological ideas. His skill is not just in breaking down the technical nuances but also in turning them into captivating stories that appeal to a wide range of people.

Enthusiasm for Gadgets: Chris's passion for gadgets comes through in everything he writes. He enthusiastically navigates the fast-paced world of innovation, covering everything from wearables to smartphones to cutting-edge tech trends, making sure his readers stay educated and empowered in an era of rapid technological progress.

Highlights of Publications: Chris Amber is the author of several critically acclaimed books that explore various facets of technology and gadgets. His books are guides that lead readers on a thrilling voyage through the intriguing nexus of human life and technical growth, not just manuals.

Philosophy: Chris Amber is an advocate for universal access to technology. His writing style is centered on dissecting difficult ideas into manageable chunks so that his audience feels empowered and understood. In his view, technology is more than just a collection of devices; rather, it is a revolutionary force that is changing the way people interact with one another, live, and work.

Innovation Advocate: Chris regularly participates in the tech community outside of his writing career. He attends conferences and keeps up with the latest developments in technology. His dedication to staying current guarantees that his readers get the most up-to-date and pertinent information.

Chris Amber's books are portals to a future in which technology improves our lives rather than just being books about gadgets. Having a keen sense of creativity, Chris never stops motivating and educating others, which makes him a highly sought-after contributor to the field of technical writing.

www.ingramcontent.com/pod-product-compliance
Lightning Source LLC
Chambersburg PA
CBHW031850200326
41597CB00012B/351